Operation Attitude

• • • • • • • • • • • • • • • • •

GOD'S SECRET WEAPON: HUMOR

J. Lissner

AuthorHouse™
1663 Liberty Drive
Bloomington, IN 47403
www.authorhouse.com
Phone: 1-800-839-8640

First published by AuthorHouse 12/4/2009

ISBN: 978-1-4490-1279-3 (sc)

Printed in the United States of America
Bloomington, Indiana

This book is printed on acid-free paper.

authorHOUSE®

To my sons Will and Jake who were with me every step of the way.
May they always be blessed with the peace and joy of Christ.

A cheerful heart is good medicine, but a crushed spirit dries up the bones.

Proverbs 17:22 NIV

Chapter 1

Words cannot describe the mind-numbing fear and confusion I felt when I was diagnosed with breast cancer. At the time, I was already emotionally drained from worrying about the end of my marriage, my kids, my finances, and going back to work.

I still had my faith, but as the year dragged on, my situation felt more and more precarious. I wasn't even carrying my own health insurance. That was through my soon to be ex-husband's company. I was frazzled and discouraged. I prayed tearfully for Christ to help me find the peace and joy Scripture promises. And what did I hear?

"Conehead."

"I have seen what a laugh can do. It can transform almost unbearable tears into something bearable, even hopeful." —Bob Hope

I couldn't see any connection between my struggles and some crazy comedy about aliens with heads shaped like cones. How could that be God's answer to my coping with cancer? I kept getting an image of me sitting in the treatment room wearing a conehead. I continued to ask God what looking and acting like a fool could possibly accomplish.

It took me awhile to accept this as The Almighty's solution. For obvious reasons, I thought I'd misinterpreted the message. Discernment can be very difficult in prayer. I prayed again and again. One word kept coming to mind. "Conehead." I thought the chemotherapy drugs were causing serious side effects. Yet, still I got, "Conehead." Day after day, I received the same stupid answer.

Finally I figured I'd give the Old Boy the benefit of the doubt. I purchased a conehead and some crazy wigs and wore them to my cancer treatments. The goofy outfits helped refocus my thoughts. The more positive and upbeat I was, the more positive and upbeat those around me were. It was strange, perhaps not as strange as what I was wearing, but the transformation was truly miraculous. Instead of being depressed, we were laughing together. Others may have laughed at me instead of with me, but I don't get hung up on syntax. Fun is fun and joy is joy. When you're sick or depressed, it doesn't matter where it comes from, humor can heal.

I'd never done anything outrageous before. I was relatively normal; at least I thought I was. Accepting the conehead solution was not easy, especially at a time when my entire future was questionable. Many people have similar experiences. They receive lots of major challenges all at the same time. Like me, they become overwhelmed.

For me, 1999 was a difficult year of mind-boggling portions. Yet, it turned out to be a great blessing. Not because it was easy, but because I learned how to face challenges, big and little. God works things out according to His purpose, but I have to cooperate. My part was controlling my thoughts and reactions. How I thought and acted made a huge difference—much more than I expected. I was called to use humor and a positive attitude to weather my storms of life. Through God's grace, I received joy and peace in the midst of my struggles and you can too.

I had been a stay-at-home mom for nine years when I separated from my husband in 1998. It was a pivotal time in my faith journey. I needed to learn to trust God, His love for me, and His ability to care for me. My first act of letting go was tithing. My household income dropped by two-thirds after the separation. I stayed in the same house with most of the same expenses. It seemed like a terrible time to increase giving, but I took the leap of faith anyway. I believe that is one reason I have been so blessed.

I had no desire to return to my previous career in banking. I wanted to work at home to be available for my young sons. I felt it was finally time to invest in my dream of becoming an author. I cut back everything that wasn't essential. As long as no unexpected expenses came up, I could make ends meet. Finances were tight, but I was home with my boys and publishing my first novel.

In the spring of 1999, I went in for my annual pap smear. I was feeling fine. I had no reason to see a doctor. I saw the physician's assistant instead. While I was spread-eagle in the stirrups, my PA suggested I get a baseline mammogram.

I said, "Yes," without thinking, which is what one does in that position. My first mammogram was supposed to be a baseline. It never occurred to me it would show problems. I expected to get a postcard in the mail stating my test was normal.

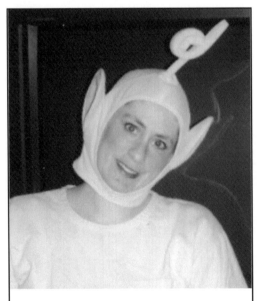

Lala the Teletubby reminds everyone to tune into fun. I channeled fun into cancer by wearing the outfits in this book from my car, through the parking lot, down the hall, in the waiting areas, throughout my treatments, and back to my car again. Some say I have a multiple personality disorder. Maybe, but I'm happy in my lunacy. Are you?

I had spent years writing my first novel. I was ecstatic to finally be not just a writer, but, drum roll…an author. One morning I was meeting a marketing man at my house. We were sitting at my dining room table. I had the phone beside me. I intended to take a call from my son's doctor and then turn off the phone.

About half an hour into the meeting, the phone rang, except it was *my* doctor's office. They had found some questionable cells on my mammogram. They wanted to schedule a biopsy to check for cancer. I was caught completely off guard. I'd never given the test a second thought. I didn't feel I could ask which breast in front of Mr. Marketing. I was too flustered to think clearly. I told him I had to take the call and ushered him out the door. So much for professionalism.

The mammogram showed a small cluster of suspicious cells. On the X-rays, they looked like a bunch of white dots, each the size of large grains of sand. I scheduled the biopsy and did some research. Ninety-seven percent of biopsies come back benign. I figured I'd take those odds. I was young. I was healthy and didn't fall into any big risk groups. Plus, my lifestyle should have reduced my chances of cancer. I never drank alcohol, never smoked, had two kids before the age of thirty, breast-fed both boys, and had no family history of breast cancer.

My only reservation was I'd heard the procedure could be painful. I called my mom. She agreed to come in town and help with my young sons after the biopsy. (I'll be referring to her as just plain, old Mom from here forward. For the sake privacy, I have given everyone in this book a pet name. Their names reflect who they are or what they do.)

The biopsy was an interesting procedure. I actually found it fascinating. It must be my minor in biology. Dr. Squeeze 'Em Up (you'll understand why I call him that in a moment) had me strapped to a table. The table was tilted until I was staring at the floor. My suspicious cells were on the left underside. The tilted position gave the doctor access to the tissue. I'm hanging there, and there was plenty hanging, I assure you. The tech put my left breast between two clear plastic mammogram plates. The plates were pressed together tightly. So I'm upside down, and what's hanging was squeezed between two plates. Comfy, huh?

Then the fun started. Directed by the mammogram image, the doctor maneuvered a needle through my breast to the questionable spots. He suctioned out a number of tissue samples. I could hear the little vacuum suctioning away. The whole procedure didn't take long. When I peeked at the petri dish, there were about twenty snakes of flesh. They looked like they came out of a small coffee stirrer.

At the end of the procedure, the nurse said she normally wrapped patients with an Ace bandage. Due to my location and exceptional size, an Ace bandage wouldn't help. I was instructed to wear a bra for twenty-four hours. I walked out absolutely fine. I could easily have taken care of my kids. I apologized to Mom for driving four hours for nothing. I wasn't the least bit concerned I had cancer. We went out to lunch and had a great time.

My follow-up visit was the following Monday. Dr. Squeeze 'Em Up examined my incision area. It was fine. We were also supposed to discuss the test results, but the pathology report had been delayed. Dr. Squeeze 'Em Up offered me another appointment to talk about the biopsy's findings. I was confident everything was fine and saw no reason to return. I told the doctor, "Call me with the results."

I enjoy writing because it requires a bazooka-sized imagination, a strong command of the English language, and an ability to weave characters in and out of the obstacle courses of life. No, I've never actually been in the military. Military personnel travel all over and people shoot at them. I do love men in uniform and have studied them extensively. (Well somebody has to do it.) The picture above is of me visiting my brother in California at Camp Pendleton for a special meet-the-Marines-and-see-what-they-do day.

Knowing my interest in the subject, BrotherTwo invited my family unit to participate. You know these guys must be brave, because they allowed me to shoot an M16, an M240 G machine gun, and throw a practice hand grenade. OK, so I exaggerated a little. We civilians were not given live ammo; the weapons were filled with blanks. Apparently heroics do not include stupidity. Anyway, back to my dream and not the dreamy.

For years I was hoping to whip my men-in-uniform fixation into a profitable lean, mean novel-writing machine. I wrote *Duty Honor Deceit*. The first in a series of books set in the military of the future. In the spring of 1999, I snapped to attention at the prospect of publishing my novel.

Finally I was through with training and ready for my first official mission. Unfortunately, I was the victim of an unprovoked enemy attack. A heartless traitor was lurking in the shadows, planting a minefield of mass destruction. This insidious enemy had no conscience, a hunger for suffering, and a willingness to take innocent victims.

I was shell shocked at the news of a breast cancer invasion. Due to the limited resources under my command, I put my writing equipment in a secure bunker. Instead I deployed an army of medical personnel to eradicate the enemy. As a prisoner of war, I had to do an about-face in my life. I discovered a ten-caliber laugh was more effective than a nuclear bomb on depression. Using positive brain brigades and an arsenal of humor, I became victorious over cancer. I won my battle, and you can too. Enter my boot camp of giggles and learn how I fought my negative attitudes.

I will never forget that short phone conversation. I was dumbfounded to hear I had breast cancer. I phoned Mom and told her the news — not the easiest call to make, because my dad had died of lymphoma years before. Mom and I didn't talk long. I only had fifteen minutes before I was due at the kids' school.

It is our family tradition that I take the boys a special lunch to school on their birthdays. FirstBorn had just turned ten. I left immediately, picked up McDonald's, and celebrated FirstBorn's "Happy Birthday Lunch." After lunch I went to SecondBorn's class and helped with the computers.

I held it together with the kids. When I came home, a friend's car was in the driveway. She had three young children and was in the process of selling her house. I had given her a key to mine. She'd gotten a surprise call from a realtor. She and her kids were at my place while hers was being shown. God provided someone to hold me and fall apart with. It was a blessing not to return to an empty house with urgent messages from my doctor's office. I was scheduled to see the general surgeon that afternoon at 3:00. I had to find someone to watch my boys after school. I called another friend. She volunteered to drive me to the doctor and arranged for her husband to pick up my kids from school.

I had previously committed to bring dinner to an older couple from church. I had a few hours to finish that meal and get ready. My friend picked me up. We dropped the dinner off early and headed to the doctor.

The general surgeon, whom I'll refer to as Dr. Cut 'Em Up, informed me I had a very early form of breast cancer called Ductal Carcinoma In Situ, or DCIS for those of us that can't pronounce medical mumbo jumbo. This was a fancy way of saying the cancer was inside individual cells and hadn't spread outside the cell walls, which was good news. It meant the cancer hadn't spread to other parts of my body.

Dr. Cut 'Em Up informed me I needed a modified lumpectomy. He would go in and remove about the size of a tennis ball from my left breast. I was not to worry about looking lopsided. He reassured me my insurance company would cover plastic surgery for an implant. I was very busty and had always wanted a reduction. Even distraught, I retorted, "If you take anything out, there is no way someone is putting it back in." I declared I would get a reduction to even things out.

The night I was diagnosed, my best friend, Nursey, came over. She held me while I cried and reassured me I would be fine. She teaches nursing and was able to answer many of the questions racing through my brain. I called on her knowledge and expertise many times.

Being diagnosed with cancer was an eye-popping experience.

I immediately started praying, and they weren't praise and thanksgiving prayers, either. Let's face it, when tragedy strikes, we aren't saying, "Thank you, God for making me miserable." I asked for help and healing, but was mostly angry with God. I felt going through a divorce was more than enough stress. But no, now I had cancer too. I had some major prayer temper tantrums. I wanted to know, "Why me?" I told God, "It's not fair!" I asked, "Where were the angels that were supposed to be protecting me?"

I wanted God to take away my problems. He didn't. Instead, God helped me through them. I had to consciously look to see His loving hand. It took days before I could feel anything besides fear and resentment. Slowly, I forced myself to count my blessings and focus on the positives.

One blessing was the whirlwind of commitments I had the day I was diagnosed. I was too busy to consider dying. By the time I left Dr. Cut 'Em Up's office, I was confident death wasn't a possibility. My cancer was detected early. The mammogram probably saved my life. The doctors speculated without the mammogram it could have taken five years to detect my cancer.

After I was diagnosed, I ran into my physician's assistant at a social event. I told her I was impressed that her office offered baseline mammograms for women under forty. Most of my younger friends were not offered baselines unless they were in a risk group. She stated her office policy was baseline mammograms at forty. I asked why she had ordered a mammogram for me since I had made no complaints and was in no risk group. She said she had a bad feeling and always listened to her instincts. Wow! To me that is nothing short of a miracle. Perhaps God had sent a few angels to watch over me.

So that was how I began my undress-from-the-waist-up journey. With breast cancer, you can toss modesty right out the door. From day one there was a long line of highly trained men who, within minutes of meeting me, were handling my breasts. The parade of practitioners who perused my plums was endless. Every single, solitary peruser agreed my cancer could not be detected through a physical exam, yet they all *felt* it was necessary to check.

In addition to Dr. Cut 'Em Up, I had three other main doctors: Dr. Shape 'Em Up (the plastic surgeon); Dr. Drug 'Em Up (the chemotherapy oncologist); and Dr. Burn 'Em Up (the radiation oncologist). Naturally, all four chosen by my insurance company were men. Each and every one of them, plus mammogram takers, technicians, nurses, various extra doctors, and, as far as I can tell, everyone else on the planet, has seen and thoroughly examined my breasts. I sincerely appreciate their thoroughness and concern throughout my long and painful journey.

"From there to here, from here to there, funny things are everywhere."
—Dr. Seuss

For I know the plans I have for you, declares the Lord, plans to prosper you and not to harm you, plans to give you hope and a future.

JEREMIAH 29:11 NIV

Chapter 2

The next few weeks were a big blur. I had three more doctors to see. It was impossible to absorb all the information. The purpose of surgery is to remove known groups of cancer cells. The goal of radiation is to kill any local cells left in the area. Chemotherapy is designed to kill systemic cells, meaning it destroys stray cells that traveled through the blood to other parts of the body.

I took another person to each doctor's appointment because I was receiving so much information. My secretary for the day took notes, which freed me up to listen and ask questions. SisterOne surprised me by flying into town and attending the first two-hour meeting with the oncologist. She took pages of notes about the risks, side effects, and survival rates for each of my options. Obviously it was very important to get those facts right. The notes were a big help later when I had to sort out the pros and cons of each option and make treatment decisions.

The plastic surgeon was concerned about my breast reduction request. Not because I wasn't large enough, but because he didn't want me making a "big" decision under duress and regretting it later. He asked how long I had considered a reduction. I told him, "Twenty years." He was comfortable after that. I may have hated cancer, but the reduction surgery was a thankful bonus.

After visiting all the doctors and reviewing my options, I formed a plan of attack. Dr. Cut 'Em Up would perform a modified lumpectomy. He would leave me open. Dr. Shape 'Em Up would follow with the much-desired bilateral breast reduction. If the pathology didn't show any surprises, and nobody expected it would, I would finish with radiation for a total of three months of treatment. No chemotherapy would be necessary because there was no invasive cancer.

Next came the hard part: telling my boys. FirstBorn was just ten and SecondBorn only seven. I was in the process of getting a divorce, so the kids had a counselor. I called her. I didn't want the boys hearing the word "cancer" and thinking I was going to die. They had enough insecurity in their lives. I told their father (hereafter called Ex) and the four of us went to the counselor together.

Help! We've tripped on a bad year and we're falling into trouble.

We explained what the doctor found and my treatment plan. I was glad I had enlisted an expert's advice. I hadn't thought to explain who would take care of the boys while I was in treatment, but it was important for them to know. It reassured them we would all be taken care of.

The counselor emphasized to me privately that the kids would take their cues from me. Children are very sensitive to adults' emotional undertones. It was not going to be enough for me to pretend I was fine in front of the kids. I was going to have to *be* fine, or the unknown fears they sensed would affect them.

I'm smiling because you're my Mom and I'm laughing because there is nothing you can do about it.

✳✳✳

I'm from a large family of eight kids. Mom had planned a family reunion in June for her children, their spouses, and the grandchildren; a small gathering of 36 of my closest relatives. The doctors felt there were no reasons for me to miss it. My surgery was scheduled for immediately after the reunion on June 22, 1999.

We had a wonderful vacation at Fripp Island, a 3,000-acre private island in South Carolina. Somehow, there was a major mix-up, and my family and BrotherThree's family were *forced* to stay in a luxury condo a block away. Our house was known as the "quiet" house, which is a relative term when there are 36 relatives traipsing through and 21 of those are children. The other two condos were right on the ocean. Every day we trotted down the back steps, onto the beach, and into the surf. We had a marvelous time playing in the sand, riding the waves, and swimming.

We also had plenty of quality family interactions that fostered love and interdependence. For example, all the kids were instructed to bring their Star Wars light sabers. The battles between the forces of good and evil were endless, although it was difficult to tell which was which in any given duel.

At night, people converged on our "quiet" house and attempted to conquer the world in the board game Risk. They yelled, screamed, groaned, and cheered as treaties were made and broken; the weak ganged up on the strong; armies were destroyed; and world conquest was finally achieved. What better way to promote family bonding than through saber fights and mock wars?

We also had daily devotionals and prayed together. Some of the adults gave presentations. I spoke about my fears and how God provided me with a special verse for reassurance: Jeremiah 29:11, "For I know the plans that I have for you, declares the Lord, plans to prosper you and not to harm you, plans to give you hope and a future."

I was confident this verse was specifically for me because God kept repeating it. First, I purchased a small poster with that verse on it and hung it in my bathroom. Then my sister sent me a plaque with Jeremiah 29:11. It was read at church. I got a greeting card and a prayer card with that verse, all within weeks. It was like the Holy Spirit was saying, "Hello, this verse is for you. Trust me." I still have the plaque hanging in my house.

Our week of R&R was a great preparation for the months ahead. It was a fun distraction. Most importantly, everyone was very supportive. I was going to be lifted up in prayer by lots of people who loved me. I didn't feel I was entering the cancer zone alone.

Don't be concerned about the outward beauty that depends on jewelry, or beautiful clothes, or hair arrangement. Be beautiful inside, in your hearts.

1 Peter 3:3-4a LAB

Chapter 3

When the fun and frolic was over, I returned for my operation. Mom drove into town, and this time it was necessary. We arrived at the hospital early. In the surgery area I was dressed in an exquisite gown. My designer creation was made of lightweight cotton with a delicate blue and white print. It hit fashionably above the knee and had a revealing slit up the back with two ties for a cool and refreshing feel. I was also given jewelry: a white bracelet engraved with my name. To complete the outfit, I was given a matching white blanket. I used the blanket as a shawl to cover my backside when I strolled along the hospital promenade.

A model patient.

Once properly attired, I was escorted down the hall for another date with Dr. Squeeze 'Em Up. Because my cancer cells were microscopic and scattered, it would be impossible for the surgeon to see the culprits. Dr. Squeeze 'Em Up's special brand of torture was to mark the area for removal. First the cancerous area — i.e., my boob — was again placed in the high-tech mammogram machine. I was tilted, and the two plates were pressed tightly together. As if this contortion wasn't uncomfortable enough, Dr. Squeeze 'Em Up forced (I assure you, my body didn't take it willingly) a thin metal wire into my breast and guided it around the cancerous cells. "Ouch!" doesn't begin to describe it.

He left some extra wire hanging out of my breast attached to a plastic doohickey. Obviously once in place, it was extremely important the wire and doohickey didn't move. Stabilization required an expensive, specially designed device. The nurse carefully extracted a white Styrofoam coffee cup from a stack on the counter. She placed it over the doohickey and taped the cup to my breast. I was redressed for my stroll back to the surgery area.

As the belle of the ball, I was escorted through the halls sporting the extra attachment underneath my lovely designer hospital gown. Trust me, a hospital gown does not camouflage a cup taped to your breast. At this pivotal point I decided I needed a personal motto. I quickly adopted one and clung to it throughout my treatments. I would encourage you to memorize it. Repeat it any time you are in a cup-sticking-from-your-breast type situation. I mumbled my motto, "Dignity, always maintain dignity," as I held my head high and marched forward donning the doctor's latest addition to my fashion ensemble.

Kiss that bad attitude good-bye.

In the pre-op area, I was given an IV. I have never taken medications well and have a history of being highly sensitive to drugs. I was sitting on the bed with my feet dangling over the edge. The nurse put something in my IV. She barely got the needle out before I was so dizzy and nauseated I fell sideways on the bed. From what I heard, I looked like a big tree going timmmberrr.

The nurse immediately offered to give me something to settle my queasy stomach. She barely got the "anti-nausea" medication in the IV before I vomited. She kindly offered to give me something different. From my prone position, I growled sternly, "Don't you dare put anything else in that IV."

Once stable I was taken to surgery. I was in surgery about six hours. I had 350 to 400 stitches, 22 staples, and basting stitches around the nipples. Oddly enough, the insurance company considered that outpatient surgery. They did permit me twenty-three hours of extended recovery in a hospital bed.

"We don't laugh because we're happy — we're happy because we laugh." —William James

I spent most of that time in a drug-and-pain-induced state. That evening, Nursey came to visit. I greeted her by vomiting. Fortunately she is trained for that sort of thing and handled it beautifully.

All I could think was "Dang (or something close to it) this stinks." There were plenty of moments when I felt more dangnified than dignified. At those times, I tried to focus on the positive and forget the rest. If you want to increase your prayer life, just go though a serious illness. I promise it will bring you to your knees. It certainly did for me.

That night, I drifted in and out of consciousness. In the middle of the night, I remembered that when drugs make me queasy, food settles my stomach. I was determined to stop dry heaving because it's painful to puke with fresh sutures. I buzzed the nurse. She raised the top of the bed to about thirty degrees, which was as much as my bandaged chest could comfortably take. The hospital table was positioned above my chest. I was given a dish of Jell-O and a spoon. Once I was set, the nurse scurried off to help another patient.

Because I only had outpatient surgery, she assumed I could feed myself, but I encountered some technical difficulties. I couldn't lift my head. I was too nauseated to wear my glasses and couldn't see without them. Plus the medication was affecting my depth perception and coordination. After a number of failed attempts, I quit trying to use the spoon. It was just too complicated.

I was determined to eat the Jell-O and stop the pukes. With my hand shaking, I reached up to the table. Even that small movement was painful after chest surgery. I felt my way inside the bowl and picked up the cubes of Jell-O with my fingers. I struggled to eat the wiggly gelatin. Between the medications, the pain, and the slippery nature of the food, my aim was terrible. I got as much in my hair as I did in my stomach.

Later that night, I felt slightly better and requested crackers. Dang, those little cracker packages are hard to open without moving your arms. A kind soul from housekeeping noticed me struggling, opened the crackers, and moved the table closer to my mouth. I was able to maneuver the crackers into my mouth, and ate a number of packages. I could feel the crumbs being magnetically drawn to the Jell-O in my hair. By morning my hair felt like thick, sticky clumps of dried noodles. Fortunately, I was too sick and miserable to care.

Mom came to pick me up that afternoon. I still wasn't able to lift my head. She was terrified to take me home in that condition. The nurse agreed. I was "allowed" an extra few hours in the hospital while they changed my medication. I believe I stayed an extra two or three hours. Boy, did I take advantage of that insurance company or what?

I returned home and spent the next few days living downstairs. It was too painful to lie down in a bed and unthinkable to get back up. I sat in the recliner and drifted in and out of consciousness. Once I got off the medication, I recovered quickly. It seems prescription pain pills are actually puke pills for me. Nursey came over to my house, changed my dressing, and helped me wash the gelatin and cracker clumps out of my hair.

By the beginning of the following week, I thought the worst was behind me. I was able to rest and sometimes even sleep in bed. My days were spent in the recliner with a pillow pressed against my chest. I steadily improved. Mom and I were both eager to hear the pathology report. When the call came from Dr. Cut 'Em Up, Mom could tell, even before I got off the phone, it was bad news.

"Don't take life too seriously. You'll never get out alive." —Elbert Hubbard

Spend your time and energy in the exercise of keeping spiritually fit. Bodily exercise is all right, but spiritual exercise is much more important and is a tonic for all you do. So exercise yourself spiritually and practice being a better Christian, because that will help you not only now in this life, but in the next life too.

1 TIMOTHY 4:7B-8 LAB

Chapter 4

The pathology report revealed a surprise. The tissue removed had additional areas of noninvasive cancer and a small area of invasive cancer. I would need to return to surgery. The doctor would remove a cluster of lymph nodes to determine if the cancer had metastasized. This was the scariest time. My mind raced to life and death. Contained cancer in my chest was one thing; invasive cancer attacking other parts of my body was quite another.

Mom was a real trooper. I was not up for telling dozens of people. Mom made most of the calls and everyone began praying again. I had requested no one visit who could not stay positive. It was a challenge for both of us. We focused on what could be done and not the "what ifs." I've learned what ifs drag me down into a pit of hopelessness and despair that is difficult to crawl out of. I spent hours in prayer and meditation. Mom and I also went to Mass together daily.

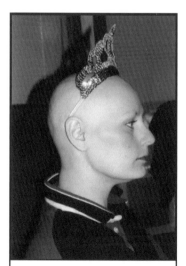

Queen Billiard going to the Cue Ball to declare cancer a royal pain.

The doctor's office immediately called my insurance company. My second surgery was approved for the following Tuesday, July 6, 1999. Because I didn't schedule too far in advance, the nurse said my surgery would be late in the day. Everyone wants surgery early because you're not allowed to eat after midnight. It's not a huge life-and-death issue, but it makes for a long day. I guess God figured I could use a break.

The nurse called with my surgery time. I was originally scheduled for a late afternoon appointment. When she gave the hospital clerk my name, it was an old neighbor of mine. Miraculously an early morning appointment became available. I would not spend a whole day hungry and scared. The early time felt like a whisper from God telling me He was listening and He cared. I informed Ex of the date and time. The two of us arranged our schedules to accommodate the children.

The lymph node dissection really was an outpatient procedure. It took less than an hour. Dr. Cut 'Em Up scooped out a cluster of lymph nodes from under my left arm. I still have numbness under my arm and across my chest where my nerves were cut. I was home by noon. I dragged myself upstairs to bed and Mom went to fill the doctor's prescription. She returned hesitant to disturb me with more bad news.

My health insurance was carried through Ex's company. The pharmacy said it had been canceled. No medical insurance was not what I needed to hear hours after a second cancer surgery with a life-threatening illness looming over my head. I decided the problem was a bureaucratic mistake, and would deal with it later when I was more coherent. Unfortunately, it was not that simple.

Ex is a worker's compensation attorney. He deals regularly with doctors and insurance companies coordinating health benefits and settling worker's claims. Our formal legal separation agreement stated he was required to carry my health insurance until the divorce was final. I was still listed as his spouse on the policy, so all correspondence went to him. He was supposed to forward insurance information to me.

Days later, after numerous calls, I figured out my medical insurance problem. Ex had not told me his company changed insurance carriers on July 1. My second surgery was preapproved by the wrong insurance company before they had entered the cancellation order in their computer. The new company did not cover unapproved surgeries.

Bloom where you're planted. Some of the rarest, most prized flowers grow in poor soil and desolate places. Keep watering the seeds of happy thoughts while weeding out the negative ones.

Don't ignore problems or pretend they don't exist. That won't make them go away. Just like in a garden, unattended weeds spread and choke out what should be growing. Nip your challenges and negative thoughts in the bud.

We'll never get rid of all the weeds in our lives, but if you keep digging up the emotional dandelions they won't choke out the light. Be certain you're using good compost. Don't let someone else's manure fertilize anger, frustration, or bitterness in you.

If you work on your attitude garden, your life will produce a beautiful bouquet.

I contacted Ex. He sent the following e-mail on July 12, 1999: "There are several issues we need to address about health insurance. I did not want to bring these up while you were in the midst of your surgery and biopsy.

"Our health insurance…switched as of July 1. There are some claim forms you are supposed to use until we all get our new insurance cards and I'll bring you some tonight.

"I didn't think of the switch until after the 4th of July. I woke up on July 6 and realized you were having your biopsy that morning…

"Also, I have just realized that I have been paying your health insurance since we separated. You need to pay for your portion and reimburse me for what I have paid since June 1998…The difference is $146.03 (per month)."

I was more than slightly dangnified Ex hadn't mentioned the insurance switch and tried to get me to pay for the current coverage and a years worth of back premiums. There were lots of comments I wanted to make, but I'm responsible for my own behavior no matter what others are doing. God judges my motives and my actions. Peace and joy are gifts of the Holy Spirit. The Spirit cannot dwell in my heart when it's filled with hate. I calmed down and prayed; big keys to not lashing out in anger.

My sister and I used to pray on the phone together. Numerous times we prayed the armor of God from Ephesians 6:10-17. The specific words that spoke to me were, "Be strong in the Lord and in his mighty power…take your stand…(so) you may be able to stand your ground, and after you have done everything, to stand. Stand firm then."

I used to be a world-class enabler. I thought I had to ignore or allow inappropriate behaviors to be in God's will. Instead, I learned standing firm in a healthy position is not sinful. At the time, I didn't feel strong or want to stand firm. I felt weak and overwhelmed as I waited to hear if my cancer had metastasized and dealt with the insurance dilemma.

The fallout of the unknown insurance switch took almost a year to completely resolve. The easiest part was who was required to carry and pay for my health insurance. The formal separation agreement clearly stated it was Ex. I let my divorce attorney, AKA MouthPiece, deal with reiterating that and ensuring my coverage was not cancelled.

I had plenty to deal with on my end. Thankfully, I was not required to switch doctors. There was extra paperwork and phone calls with each doctor's office, the hospital, the labs, the pharmacy, and the insurance company. Most of the bills were eventually paid. A year later, the judge ordered Ex to pay for the uncovered medical bills since they were due to his negligence.

God gave us our emotions, both negative and positive. We are not expected to stop having negative feelings, but channel them in healthy, nondestructive ways and then choose not to dwell on the situations. When a hot button gets pressed, I'm instantly warped back to the previous pain. The faster I identify those negative triggers and redirect my thoughts, the less likely I am to spiral out of control. Scripture tells us to focus on what is good and right and pure. Personal desires for revenge don't fall into those categories.

"Humor is proof of faith." —Charles M. Schulz

I struggle with this constantly. If I start thinking about negative situations, it's like opening the floodgates. The more I open those doors, the more the painful thoughts pour in. My negative thoughts can drown out all the good and love around me. I have experienced over and over that my anger does give Satan a foothold. The longer I focus on what was said and done, the more my peace is destroyed.

I ask the Holy Spirit to make me instantly aware of negative triggers. Then I try to reestablish Christ's peace before I get out of control. It can be hard work and I'm not always successful. But I keep trying.

There is a big difference between wanting to change and working toward change. Everyone says they want to change negative behaviors. But talk is cheap. Working toward change implies commitment and labor. It requires time and effort.

Refocusing your thoughts is like any skill. Practice makes you better, faster, and more successful. Think of redirecting your thoughts as spiritual Olympics and Christ as your coach. I visualize Jesus in his tunic, with a stopwatch and a whistle. When my thoughts become negative and unhealthy, he blows the whistle. I jump out of the blocks. The faster I refocus my thoughts, the faster I get to the finish line of peace and joy. I used to be slow and often couldn't finish for days or weeks. Now I'm a good sprinter and finish in minutes or hours.

The reality is we can never get away from our thoughts. Our minds are constantly racing. The question is are you going to run short sprints or grueling marathons? The choice is yours. Just remember, whether we like it or not, everybody is entered in the race.

If your life is running smoothly, a few marathons here and there are manageable. However, when major stress hits, the negative triggers may start your mind racing, ten, twenty, fifty, hundreds of times a day. If you're running sprints and leaning on your coach, you'll be tired, but not spent. If you're running marathons, or worse you never get off the track, you'll be physically exhausted and emotionally drained.

Satan loves to enter people in marathons. He focuses on weak competitors he can trick into running the same mental race for weeks, months, even years. It takes hard work and commitment to become spiritually buff and stay fit, but that's what we're called to do. Why? Because the faithfully buff are happier and more at peace.

World-class athletes don't workout until they achieve a certain level and then stop practicing. They have to continually exercise to maintain their fitness. Controlling our thoughts and attitudes is not something we achieve and then have. Those muscles must be constantly worked. And like the athlete, setbacks are inevitable. That's what Coach Christ is here for. Whether our setbacks are injuries, bad days, or outside influences, our coach will guide us to the finish line. If you want to be on the medal stand, you can't quit.

When I hit emotional hurdles, instead of tripping on them, Christ helps me jump over them. He changes us from the inside out, one negative thought at a time because our thoughts determine our actions. Listen to your coach and cooperate. I used to stew for days, even weeks about a hurtful instance. As I write this, I can't remember the last time anything spiraled me into a tizzy for that long. I never go as low and I never stay there as long.

Peace is not something you can passively have and possess. You and I have to practice peace and joy to maintain it. We must be an active participant in our faith process. You too can achieve mental tranquility and joy. Go for the gold. It is a priceless medal you'll be proud to wear.

If you want to be head and shoulders above the competition, listen to Coach Christ.

✳✳✳

One other tidbit about the node dissection: I came home with a drain, an extra attachment shaped like a hand grenade. The grenade was attached to a clear tube that was inserted under my left arm. My sons were fascinated with it. They watched the blood and bits of flesh drain into my grenade. They gave unsuspecting visitors a play-by-play of what it looked like and how I emptied it. Oh, the joys of post-op life.

Nothing makes you more dependent on God's strength than pathology reports. Waiting for the test results felt like an eternity. I tripped over a few worry hurdles that week. When I fell, I tried to go to prayer. I jumped every time the phone rang. This time it was good news and bad news. My lymph nodes were cancer-free. Yeah! The problem was my original pathology had shown invasive cancer and the doctors weren't sure they had removed it all.

Doctors like to see a half-inch clear margin. That means they removed a half an inch of healthy tissue around the cancerous area. This ensures no cancer is left in the body. Cancer cells are microscopic and you only need to leave one to restart the process. My clear margin was less than a sixteenth of an inch.

Usually in my situation, the general surgeon goes in and removes a little more tissue just to be safe. Unfortunately, the plastic surgeon operated after the general surgeon. The plastic surgeon had cut out a great deal of tissue. He had also cut off my nipples and reattached them. With all the shifting of flesh, there was no possibility of returning to the original cancer location and cutting out a little more. My margin wasn't crystal clear, but gray and murky. Plus, with invasive cancer, there is always the possibility a stray cancer cell traveled in the blood to another organ.

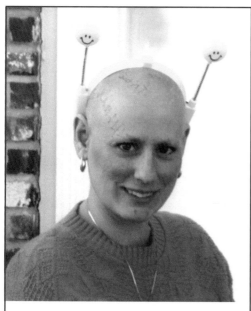

"Laugh at yourself first, before anyone else can." —Elsa Maxwell'

I was left with a dilemma. Only undergo radiation and hope that killed everything or add chemotherapy and know it was gone. If I underwent chemo, the reoccurrence rate would be less than five percent and as low as three percent. I had a lot to consider. This huge life-altering decision was made at the same time the insurance fiasco was going on. I felt attacked from all sides. Even my own body was against me.

I cannot fathom going through this scary a decision without prayer — lots and lots of it, my own and everybody else's. I had been a regular at daily Mass for years. In 1999 I went, dare I say, religiously. My major concern was my boys. What was best for them? Given my propensity to puke on any medication, my fear of high-powered chemotherapy drugs was astronomical. It would be hard for my young sons to watch me become bald, sick, and incoherent. On the other hand, generally if cancer returns, it returns with a vengeance. The survival rate for reoccurring cancer is significantly lower. Skipping chemo not only decreased my survival rate, it increased the possibility of going through the whole experience again.

Out of fear, I wanted so much to say no to chemotherapy, but I couldn't. I concluded a sick mom for months was better than a dead one. My family and friends all offered to help. The boys and I would be taken care of. Reluctantly, I chose to undergo chemotherapy.

If my children had been grown, I could easily have made a different decision. God gave me a peace about my choice. I was terrified, but certain it was the correct decision for my family. Even when our choices are difficult and opposed to what we want, we can be at peace with any decision that is in God's will. He sees far beyond what we do. That's why His choices are best.

The one thing I want from God, the thing I seek most of all, is the privilege of meditating in his Temple, living in his presence every day of my life, delighting in his incomparable perfections and glory.

Chapter 5

My father had been a plastic surgeon who did his share of boob jobs. I'd never given this much thought. Throughout my treatment I had lots, and I do mean lots, of breast exams. Every place I went started with, "Undress from the waist up." The plastic surgeon's exam was different from the others. Everyone else gave me the standard flat-fingered breast exam. The plastic surgeon needed a *feel* for the tissue.

He squeezed my breasts all around to determine the density. He bobbled them up and down. I guess he was checking my flop factor. He flicked my nipples with his pointer finger and verified if I could feel it, both before and after the surgery. He measured everything. He took before and after naked frontal and side-view pictures of my breasts. The day of the surgery, before the cup was taped to my breast, he took a marker and drew cutting lines all over my chest. Nude photos, nipple flicking, squeezing, and breast marking was not exactly my idea of maintaining modesty. Those were definitely moments when I was more dangnified than dignified.

"Your living is determined not so much by what life brings to you as by the attitude you bring to life." —John Miller

I chuckled as I pictured my dad doing thorough breast exams, boob markings, and nude photos. I decided to share my reflections with Dr. Shape 'Em Up at an opportune moment. I went to have the staples and basting sutures removed. I was on the table, undressed from the waist up, of course. The doctor was removing the basting sutures around my nipples. As he pulled, I arched off the table in pain. It was the perfect time for some comic relief. I squeaked out the words, "You know, Doc, now that I've experienced how you examine, photograph, and mark your patients, I can see why my dad always said he enjoyed being a plastic surgeon."

Most of my incisions healed nicely. There were a few spots underneath my breasts where the incisions were white and weepy. Those spots needed more air. Time for more dangnity. When my boys were at school or their dad's, I was alone.

To air my breasts, I ran around topless. Even then part of my breasts laid over the weepy incisions. I sat topless, completely reclined in the chair with my arms over my head. That provided ample airing. Heck, I even fell asleep like that. I sent my family a group e-mail telling them I was considering joining Nudistcolony.com. In case you're visualizing this as remotely sexy, it wasn't. With the scars around my chest I looked more like the bride of Frankenstein than Pamela Anderson.

Conehead consumes mass quantities of chemo.

Slowly I healed. When I was dressed, I wore a loose sports bra. I wasn't able to wear a regular bra for months, and then only for short periods of time. The scars on the left side were tender for years. I couldn't catch a ball against my chest or have anything hit me there. The right side was much better because it wasn't subjected to as much abuse.

✳✳✳

I've learned never to tell a cancer doctor, "I'm feeling fine." In physician's lingo that translates to, "Great, I'm ready for the next torture session." They always want you feeling better before they make you sick again. My whole process went this way.

They wouldn't do the second surgery until I'd healed enough from the first. They wouldn't start chemo until I'd healed enough from the second surgery. They wouldn't start the next chemo treatment until I was feeling better from the previous one. They wouldn't start radiation until I recovered from chemo. Basically the entire year was a series of struggles to regain my health so I could be made sick again. You can bet by December, if a doctor asked me how I was feeling, I said, "Terrible. Absolutely horrible."

That August I'd healed enough from the surgeries to begin chemotherapy. My first chemo experience was on August 5, 1999. I sat in the treatment room with five to ten other patients. Like the other poor slugs in attendance, I was scared. I was the youngest lab rat participating. We were each hooked up to an IV with our "drug of choice" dripping into our blood.

They kept the IV solutions and drugs in the refrigerator, just to make the experience more appealing. I was scheduled for doses of A&C, or Adriamycin and Cytoxan (note the "toxan," AKA "toxin" in the drug's name). The first drug was red. A nurse took a syringe and slowly pushed the red liquid into my IV. What goes in red comes out red for days. The other cocktail was in a bag attached to my IV. For two to three hours that ice-cold concoction was dumped into my veins. I was freezing. I brought a jacket and still asked for one blanket and then another.

As I sat shivering, I observed my fellow honorees. They were depressed to have what is essentially poison pumped into their veins. The doctors call it chemotherapy, but don't let them fool you. Those of us who have had chemo know exactly what it is. Poison. Why do you think our hair falls out? It's because chemo kills lots of cells. Like the other contestants, I was painfully aware I was taking home a booby (no pun intended) prize: a six-day, seven-night trip to the bathroom of my choice.

OK, so fun-filled adventures do not start at the oncologist's office. The room reeked of hopelessness. I wanted to remain upbeat. I figured why ruin this moment in my life for a lousy moment in the future? I would have plenty of time to be miserable. For weeks I had been reminding myself not to worry about my post-chemo reactions. Prepare, yes; worry, no, because worrying accomplishes nothing.

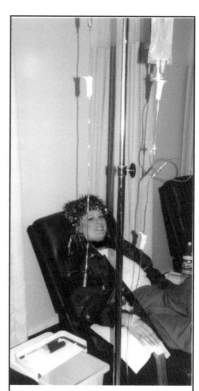
Bellied up to the chemo bar.

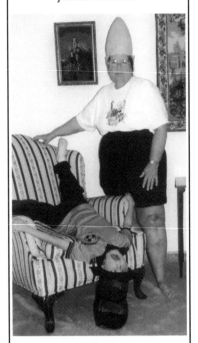

Mom and SecondBorn
join in the fun.

"Momentary fits of insanity
help prevent brain damage."
—Dr. Harvey Mindness

How did I prepare? With humor and prayer. Cancer treatments and other medical maladies are not fun. Neither is being jobless, losing a loved one, a car breaking down, money problems, and the many other stresses we face.

When I have a problem, I first look for solutions, but for many calamities, no solution exists. We simply have to accept them. I can't bring a person back from the dead. (If you can, give me a call. I could use your services.) Logically, if we can't change a situation and there are no answers, then our only options for peace and joy are to alter our attitudes and reactions.

The first attitude adjustment I needed was in trusting God and His love for me. God had been working on this issue with me for a while. When people violate our trust and don't keep their promises, we tend to project that untrustworthiness onto God. I made that mistake and still have to fight that tendency.

When we feel we're being treated as if we have no value and our needs don't matter, Satan whispers that we are unlovable and God doesn't care. Too many faithful Christians have no sense of God's love for them and therefore can't trust Him completely. I know because I was one of them. I spent hours reading Scripture, doing Bible studies, attending church, serving others, and praying, yet I frequently cried myself to sleep because I felt so unloved. I was a Christian without ever knowing Christ's love: completely saved without the here-and-now benefits of abiding peace and ongoing joy.

At the start of the divorce process, I was an emotional mess. I went on a five-day retreat. I browsed the retreat center's bookstore and felt drawn to purchase a booklet on meditation. Later, I met with a priest. I prayed about the meeting beforehand. I begged God to speak to me through the priest, to show me that He loved me and cared about me. Not in a general Christ-loves-everyone sort of way, but me specifically, right then as I was.

I spoke and prayed with the priest. He had no idea I'd purchased the mediation booklet. At the end, he paused. He appeared perplexed and hesitantly asked, "Have you ever heard of meditation?" It was obviously not something he regularly suggested.

The priest instructed me to read 1 John 4:16, about God's love before meditating. "God loves me" became my mantra. The priest told me to repeat that during meditation and throughout the day until it became as natural as breathing.; until I felt it and believed it. That process took over a year.

I had told God I needed a neon sign in the sky with a clear message. He gave me one. The sign said, "Meditation. You will learn of My love through meditation."

Christ individualizes our walk with Him. Our faith journey is tailor made to account for our personalities, our strengths and weaknesses, our current needs, our past hurts, and dozens of other factors we're not aware of. In the temporal world, words and deeds don't always match, and promises and commitments are broken. Meditation was part of my answer because I needed to be healed beyond words and actions.

The purpose of meditation or centering prayer is simply to be in God's presence. It is not about speaking to the Lord or listening to His voice. The mantra or key words are used to shut out other thoughts and keep focused. What meditation does for me is best expressed in Psalm 16:1, "You have let me experience the joys of life and the exquisite pleasures of your own eternal presence."

A mother who sits and rocks her baby can communicate love as much or more than the mother who is talking. Hospitalized people often have loved ones stay with them or hold their hands. People who are dying do not want to be alone. It is often another's presence, not their words, which bring us comfort.

The meditation booklet I purchased said to imagine sitting on God's lap or being held in the palm of His hand. Then quietly stay there. I had to learn to relish being with the Lord with no expectations on either side. I didn't have to earn Christ's love, and I had to accept that He loved me regardless of my circumstances.

The way I meditate is individualized to meet my needs. It was vital for me to feel Christ's physical presence, to feel safe while He held me. I don't know how I got started meditating the way I do. My system certainly isn't the way the booklet suggested.

I turn my electric blanket on high, get in bed under another blanket and a comforter, and surround myself with pillows. The weight and the warmth simulate being held. I ask the Holy Spirit to go to the places I need to be healed. The places I can't identify or don't know about. Cocooned in bed, I close my eyes and revel in God's presence. Do I fall asleep? No. It defies logic, but God's solutions often do.

I'd been meditating over a year when I had my first chemo treatment. Our image of God should constantly be growing and evolving. By August of 1999, I had a sense of God's love and was in my infancy of trusting Him. I was very ill after chemo and spent lots of time in bed. My mind was disjointed and I was in the bathroom constantly. I meditated some, but spent more time in traditional prayer.

I told God I was worried about my boys. It seemed we were all hurting so much. I kept asking how we were supposed to get through all this. As I said earlier, my answer was, "Conehead." I was being told to stir things up, to add fun in the midst of my suffering, not change my situation, only the way I went through it.

And stir things up I did. It took me awhile to find a conehead. The "rooster," as Mom calls the wig to the right, was my original outfit. I sported this classic look to my second chemo treatment.

At the beginning, I had a hard time trusting God's answer. His solution seemed downright stupid. Scripture has numerous examples of "stupid" answers to complex problems: "David, see that big giant, Goliath, you can take him buddy;" "Gideon a hundred against one, go for it;" "Joshua, blow your trumpets while walking your army around Jericho, and you'll conquer the city." Dumb, dumb, and dumber, and yet they all worked. Why? Because God wants us to give Him the credit. Conehead was my answer because then there would be no question whose idea it was. Wearing costumes to treatment would not have been in my first five million solutions.

"In life, pain is inevitable, but suffering is optional."

—Hedy Schleifer

I wasn't initially comfortable with the whole conehead idea. Just telling family members and friends what I planned to do was embarrassing. I was certain everyone would stare and make fun of me. I was self-conscious wearing multicolored eyelashes and a spiked wig through the parking lot, in the elevator, and in the waiting room.

At the first treatment, Dr. Drug 'Em Up told me I would lose my hair and recommended I get a wig. The next time I saw him I was bald and wearing the rooster. He gave me a rather strange look and questioned my attire.

I reminded him, "Doc, you told me to buy a wig, but you weren't very specific." I batted my eyes at him. "I even added matching eyelashes just for you."

He laughed, but dressing up wasn't really fun until I got to the treatment room. Once everyone started laughing and talking, it was a blast. The other patients' enthusiastic responses hooked me. People were giggling and joking instead of being depressed.

My outfits didn't change anybody's future. The silly diversions just made their present condition more bearable. And that's what Christ does for us: He makes the unbearable, bearable. He's in the midst of our pain, to help us through it. We can experience His love, peace, and joy while the world is crumbling around us. The catch is we have to do our part. We have to focus on Christ and not our troubles. We have to accept situations and solutions we don't like or think will work.

By my next treatment, I'd found and wore the conehead. Dr. Drug 'Em Up heard my voice and called out, "Is that patient having another bad hair day?"

His nurse replied, "You've gotta see this."

He peeked around the corner, saw the conehead, and shook his head. He asked if I'd purchased a "normal" wig.

I told him I had no idea what he meant.

His response, "Brown, something that looks like hair."

I'm in the Lord's army and I salute my Commander and Chief

Some people have no imagination. Throughout my treatments, he teased me. He also told me that he and the other patients were counting on me to continue my antics. The fact is, if life knocks you flat on your back, you only have two choices: you can take it lying down or you can look straight up. Talk to your good buddy, God. He will offer you solutions you've never dreamed of based on who you are and what you need.

Don't worry; most people aren't called to be a public idiot. That was special just for me. It addressed my situation and my needs. Finding costumes and writing vignettes gave me a creative outlet with a purpose. The silly distractions refocused my thoughts. Instead of thinking about how I was feeling, or more accurately not feeling, I spent time conjuring up outfits. I invested hours in writing goofy comments. I also had to find, buy, or make the items. When I was awake and coherent — coherent being a relative term — I spent lots of time preparing to dress up. That left very little time to mope.

It was miraculous to see the transformation in myself, my family, the doctors and staff, and the other patients. Once I started acting goofy, those deeply "religious" thoughts kept me going. When I stopped being frightened and paranoid, so did my boys. When I was in those treatment rooms, no one was downcast or bored. I got the place hopping. People became lively and animated. I had little old ladies in the conehead, giggling as they dragged their IV poles around. I can honestly say I had fun with cancer, not from cancer, but with it.

Cancer and other life challenges aren't jokes. I'm not suggesting you make fun of suffering. You don't need to minimize pain to maximize joy. You too can learn to consume mass quantities of fun, and you don't have to wear a conehead to do it. Pray for the help to stay positive and find laugher. Both distress and joy can be contagious. Be sure you're spreading the right one.

Long after I started spreading the giggles, I understood it was a ministry: a way for me to give even when I was sick. It also addressed an underlying issue that had been gnawing at me: I hated being needy. I'd always been a giver and a doer for others. Now it was my turn, and I didn't like feeling helpless and weak. Remaining positive and projecting that image gave me a focus, a goal, and a purpose.

Upon reflection, I'm dangnified by my vocation. When other people are called to serve God, they get things like feed the poor, house the homeless, or care for orphans. Me, what do I get? "Conehead." What God-given talent was I called upon to share? I have the ability to make a complete idiot out of myself in public. "Gee, thanks, Lord."

I am the bread of life. I myself am the living bread come down from heaven. If anyone eats this bread he shall live forever.

John 6:48, 51a NA

Chapter 6

My months in chemotherapy can be summed up with uhh, duh, huh, what? I remember almost nothing and was regularly confused. It was a drug-induced blur. I will relay what I wrote in my journal and e-mails. There are also snippets I remember, but they're in no particular order, because I don't know the order. This portion may be random, difficult to follow, and disjointed, but that's how my life was.

Chemotherapy was, by far, the hardest part to get psyched to endure. After chemo I was so disoriented I bumped into walls. When I was in treatment, it was hard to stay positive in between trips to the toilet. Some days the mere act of standing up was challenging. I crawled up the stairs when I was too weak to stand or so nauseated I was afraid I'd fall.

One night a woman from church delivered dinner. After I opened the door, I became dizzy. I stumbled into the wall, leaned against it, slid down to the floor, and put my head between my knees. I could not even stand to thank her for the meal.

It was scary going to chemo knowing the above would follow. I have no idea how people without faith get through it. I generally have low blood pressure, but fear elevated it. One day before treatment my blood pressure was unusually high. When the nurse commented on it, I pointed to the chemo room and said, "I've been in there and I know what's coming. Heck yeah, my heart is racing."

***

Dr. Drug 'Em Up scheduled my chemo appointments for Thursdays. He originally stated I would feel like I had a bad flu for a few days. I would be sick, but not incapacitated. The original plan was for a family member to stay with me from Thursday through Sunday. That was the theory.

Unfortunately I flunked chemotherapy. I know other survivors who had the same A&C treatments. They were sick, but not down and out like I was. As I've said, I do not do drugs well. It doesn't take much for me to get the benefits or side effects from medication.

Dr. Drug 'Em Up wanted to keep an eye on my progress with weekly blood tests. My white blood cell count was expected to slowly drop with each additional treatment. The goal was to keep the count dropping, but not let it fall below 1,000. Great plan, Doc. My first post-chemo blood test count was 200. Oops.

This is how I usually looked: pale and pathetic. On the bad days, Nursey and other friends would come over and check on me.

"There's not much fun in medicine, but there's a lot of medicine in fun." —Josh Billings

Professionals often suggest writing letters to those who frustrate us. I thought this was an excellent idea. Of course I wrote it Lissner style, because being silly stopped me from playing dead... literally.

Yapp E. Pooch
1 Chew Toy Circle
Gonna BE 88888

Dear Dr. Wolfe,

I have a bone to pick with you. My health has gone to the dogs. Since they found that spot on my mammogram, I'm so dog-tired I can't chase my tail. I pant and drool just walking up the stairs. I'm sick of putting my head in the toilet and only eating scraps from the table. Thanks to you, I've had to install a bedside fire hydrant. At night, this poor pooch howls at the moon, begging to lap up life.

It's a dog-eat-dog world out there, but after learning your new tricks, I'm not "fur"ocious enough to be leader of the pack. Instead, I put my tail between my legs and run whimpering to my bed. I just lay in my kennel licking my wounds. During the dog days of summer, I scratch at the door, longing to go for a walk in the park, chase a squirrel, or retrieve a bit of fun.

I'm bushed from this crazy dog-and-pony show. You mangy medical mutts are per"pet"ually yanking my leash and leading me from one appointment to the next. It gives me paws (pause) to think you were given a license to do this. I'm not letting sleeping dogs lie. I'm reporting you to the animal rights authorities. You're gonna be collared and sent to The Big Doghouse.

I've tried to be obedient, but you're barking up the wrong tree if you think I'm doing another K-9 blood test. If that bloodhound in the yellow lab coat comes near me, I'll bite him. I'm through with short leashes and staying put. I'm going out in the yard, rolling in the dirt, and playing fetch with my pups.

"Ruff"ly yours,

Yapp E. Pooch

I'd tried to tell this guy it didn't take much for drugs to affect me. I'd say he was a believer after that. He reduced my A&C by fifteen percent, which put it at the lowest recommended therapeutic dose. The nurse said if I had gotten even a minor infection or fever, I would have been hospitalized.

After receiving the blood test results, I went to daily Mass. My Catholic Church uses the traditional white circles of bread for the Body of Christ. I was kneeling in the pew, and the priest held up the Host. It reminded me of a white blood cell, exactly what I was lacking. After that, when I took Communion, I visualized the Body of Christ replacing my weak and cancerous cells with his own strength and vitality. I felt Jesus was healing me from the inside out, one cell at a time.

To avoid infection, the boys and I became fastidious hand washers. It's probably the only time their hands were consistently clean. I sent sanitizing washes into their classrooms. The teachers and kids routinely washed to ensure no germs were brought home.

SecondBorn managed to get strep in September. I called my doctor's office. Because my immune system was compromised, I was put on an antibiotic immediately. I got a mild case, but nothing terrible. My doctor was amazed I was never hospitalized given my blood test results, the strep, and my overall chemo experience. I attribute that to lots and lots of prayer and the healing power of humor.

Dr. Drug 'Em Up prescribed an expensive antinausea drug with numerous refills. I could take one to two pills every six hours. I took a quarter of a pill a couple of times a day. Every prescription he gave me either didn't help or had miserable side effects. We tried a number of other options. A few over-the-counter medicines seemed to work nominally, but I quickly got to a point where I took nothing additional. No, thank you. Most of the time, the medicines prescribed did more harm than good. Getting all the drugs out of my system became my primary goal.

✳✳✳

Dr. Drug 'Em Up insisted I eat to rebuild my strength. He gave me permission to consume mass quantities of anything I wanted. Finally, some medical advice I was glad to hear. After years of dieting on and off, I was being ordered to eat without restrictions or guilt. Yippy. Not!

I had a gang of outlaws (and in-laws) who cleaned the family hideout, rounded up grub, sent notes and gifts, drove the herd to school, rustled up supplies, watched the ranch, and donated to the cause. I can't say muchas gracias enough to the señors and señoritas who helped me.

There were three barriers between me and food bliss. One was a constant metal taste in my mouth that flavored everything, including chocolate. Two, I had violent, and I do mean violent, diarrhea. What went in often came out faster than the speed of light. Three, I had mouth sores. Eating with open sores in my mouth and throat was miserable. I assure you, I didn't gain weight during chemo. On the other hand, for health reasons I was determined not to lose any weight.

I had three obstacles to overcome. For the metal taste, I made a decision to ignore it. The second problem Nursey helped me with. I was trying to eat healthy. You know, fruits and vegetables. She instructed me to eat high-fat foods that constipate. She suggested cinnamon rolls and McDonald's fries. They helped the diarrhea. Ronald McDonald and I became good friends, and Nursey brought me pans of her cinnamon rolls. Another odd item that soothed my queasy stomach was a V8 Splash drink. Whatever that orange concoction was, it worked. To this day, I can't look at V8 without associating it with chemo. I'll never touch the stuff again. I've managed to get over the chemo association with cinnamon rolls and McDonald's fries. I guess I'm just determined that way.

Eating was a torturous chore with mouth sores. So much for permission to have unlimited chocolate. I didn't even want it. I would decide what quantity of metal-tasting misery I needed and force myself to eat it. A single meal took forever. I could handle only tiny bites, chew slowly, and swallow painstakingly. It was excruciating and exhausting. I'd lay my head on the table until I regained enough strength to take another bite.

I don't remember the next tidbit, but my sons are fond of retelling it. One night I fell asleep in my food. Just like on TV. I slid my face into my plate and took a nap. Yet, eat I did. Slowly, surely, bit by bit, I was able to maintain my weight. My sons did not starve either. Friends, neighbors, church members, and school parents took turns bringing meals.

I was often unable to care for myself or the boys. I don't know what I would have done without my family's constant support and encouragement. If I wasn't well enough on the Sunday following chemo to be left alone, my family member stayed, or another person came.

For example, Mom came for my third treatment. By Sunday she decided I should not be alone, but couldn't stay. While she was out grocery shopping, the doorbell rang. I opened the door. It was a friend dropping off a port-a-crib and car seat. Granted I was pretty blitzed, but I was fairly certain there wasn't a baby in the house. I learned my British sister-in-law was coming to stay. Mom had called her.

In a matter of hours, she dropped everything, packed herself and her toddler, got on a plane, and flew in to take care of my family. Mom picked her up at the airport. My friend supplied the car seat and crib. I remember almost nothing about my sister-in-law's visit except my confusion over the baby supplies arriving, but I haven't forgotten her kindness and caring. She was one of many who went out of their way to help.

When I was well enough to be left alone, I still had to care for the boys. Each weekday at about 2:30, I would evaluate myself. I'd decide if I was capable of driving the whole mile to pick up the kids. When the answer was no, someone always brought them home. For the most part, I slept while the boys were in school and tried to be alert when they were home.

How did the kids and I make it? We had tons of help from family and friends. We were blessed to experience what the Body of Christ is all about. We had people lift us up in prayer and help us with our needs. Don't let pride stop you from experiencing God's love through others. Accept help. We weren't meant to go through trials alone. God often provides for us through the hands of others.

✳✳✳

What do young boys do with a semi-lucid mother? We found creative ways to spend time together. I was often too sick for active play. The boys would spin a lightweight plastic top on my bald head (see picture to the right). Another great game involved Nerf guns. The kids would draw a bull's-eye on the back of my bald head. They'd see who could nail me the most. They had a Nerf machine gun that held thirty darts. Sometimes they would launch a surprise attack. I'd hear click, click, click, click and know one of my loving sons was pumping up the Nerf machine gun. Then a kid would bolt around the corner, Rambo style, and pelt me with darts.

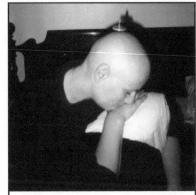

When your life is spinning out of control, always remember to keep God on top.

Many people brought or sent gifts: books, candles, lotions, perfumes, and crazy hats. SisterThree sent me a huge box of individually wrapped gifts. There were more than forty packages of trinkets, knickknacks, and whatnots. I was instructed to open a present whenever I needed a boost. They ranged from silly to cute to sweet to funny. Some days I didn't open anything. Others were a three-gift day. It was encouraging having a storehouse of surprises ready and waiting.

I'm not known for my housekeeping and was worse during treatment. SisterOne and her husband sent money for me to get my house cleaned. At the end of those days, I always felt better. I wish I could get a housecleaning boost today. As it is, I'm back to my a-little-dirt-never-hurt-anyone ways. With two boys, I find it easier to throw in the towel than scrub with it.

I joined a monthly cancer support group for women, most of whom had children at home. For me it was important to find people facing similar issues. Obviously cancer is much different for women with young children. We cannot focus totally on ourselves and our health. I never went to the group alone or had to drive myself. A close friend down the street also belonged. She or another woman drove. This was a huge blessing because I am perpetually lost, and treatment didn't improve my navigational skills.

When I joined the cancer club and spent so much time in the bathroom, I had to drink plenty of water. I drank small sips very slowly, often while lying down. Drinking lying down can be tricky. When I drank from my prone position, the water would either splash in my face, or I'd gulp. Straws worked fairly well, unless my hands were shaky, then I'd spill water on myself and the bed.

I discovered the perfect solution: bottled water with the little sports caps. When I was weak, I didn't waste the energy putting the bottle back onto the nightstand. I would just hold my baba. I could grope for it in the dark without spilling, and I didn't have to raise my head to drink it. After a while, the water bottles became a comfort item. I still carry a water baba with me regularly.

✳✳✳

Chemotherapy had many unwanted side effects. Each little fallout was a fun-filled adventure in physical misery. A "favorite" of mine was what the doctor called violent menopause. Normally estrogen levels slowly decrease over time. In my case, I went from an estrogen-producing machine to basically nil in a day. Chemo gave me all the effects of menopause instantly and intensely.

"Humor is a wonderful way to prevent hardening of the attitudes!" —Joel Goodman

The drugs strapped me into an emotional and temperature rollercoaster like the Monster of Mayhem at the amusement park. I'd feel angry at absolutely nothing and cry for no reason. I had hot flashes that swept over me like a raging fire. In a split second, my internal temperature went from normal to tropical, complete with one hundred percent humidity. I would turn beet red in the face, feel nauseated, woozy, and dizzy. I don't sweat much, but to the best of my body's ability, I would be moist all over. I often had to sit down, because I felt momentarily ill.

Not one to play favorites, I did not snub the cooler climates. I had a full range of temperature challenges, from the equator all the way to the poles. Arctic blasts were the other end of the spectrum. I'd go from normal or tropical flash to the North Pole instantly. It felt like I was standing knee deep in snow with sleet pelting my coatless body. I would be chilled to the bone, covered in goose bumps, and shaking.

During the tropical flashes, I'd peel off clothes faster than a one-minute stripper. When the Arctic blasts hit, I covered myself in blankets and sat on a heating pad underneath my electric blanket. In between, I attempted to dress normally and go about my business.

For the months during chemotherapy and immediately after, my internal temperature was a mess. Tropical flash…Arctic blast…flash…blast…flash…blast. Some days I had only a few temperature changes. On bad days I counted as many as fifty rollercoaster highs and lows. I had more tropical flashes than Arctic blasts. At night I cranked up my electric blanket one minute and kicked everything off the next.

In addition to the flash/blast syndrome, involuntarily stopping my body's estrogen production also abruptly stopped my periods. When my monthly friend returned, it did so with a vengeance. My periods became completely unpredictable. I would have premenstrual symptoms for weeks. I'd wear a pad just in case and nothing would happen. Then I would have no symptoms, and in minutes be bleeding down my legs. I had heavy periods, light periods, no periods, two periods within weeks, nothing for months, one-day periods, and three-week long periods. My body was completely confused.

By 2002 it had leveled off. I'm now a typical perimenopausal younger woman. The gynecologist predicts I'll be menopausal in a few years, but estrogen is so unpredictable. I rarely have Arctic blasts anymore. I still get bouts of tropical flashes, but not as intensely as before. They happen for days, weeks, or months, and then for no apparent reason stop. Too bad tropical flashes don't come with a beach; they'd be a lot more tolerable.

Rejoice in the Lord always! I say it again. Rejoice!

Philippians 4:4 NA

Chapter 7

Hair, especially on women, partly defines who we are. For most of my life I've had hair below my shoulders. When I was told I would lose my long locks, I resolved not to let the loss define me. I was and am more than my flowing tresses. I heard stories in the support group. Women spoke of their hair coming out in clumps on the pillow or in the shower. They said how hard it was to clean up. The doctor stated my hair would tangle and knot. It sounded messy and traumatic. I decided to take a proactive incremental approach to baldness. Before I started chemo, I got a shoulder-length bob. It was cute, sassy, and short lived.

I'm at the beauty salon preparing to join the Follically Challenged Club.

Dr. Drug 'Em Up informed me my hair would start falling out two to three weeks after my first chemo treatment. I called my hairdresser and scheduled an appointment to have my hair buzzed on day twelve.

It was summer, and my boys were not in school. When chemo made me so ill, I headed home to stay with Mom. I canceled my hair appointment. My Chicago sister-in-law arranged for me to be buzzed back home. By then, I realized how imperative my attitude was. I wanted my boys to see that losing my hair was OK with me. Hair was not the end of the world. If I got upset about being bald, they would too.

The hair buzzing became a family outing. SecondBorn requested his hair be buzzed too, as a sign of his support and unity. FirstBorn wanted no part of that. He went along as the photographer. We cracked jokes, and FirstBorn took pictures. After the stylist cut my hair I looked like G.I. Jane. Mom claims I looked cute. Yeah, right, talk about a mother's bias.

In the days that followed my scalp began to ache. I started shedding; first a little, then a lot. Mom claimed I was worse than her cat. I'd run my hand over my head, and my fingers would be covered with bits of brown hair. It didn't fall out evenly. I had huge bald spots intermixed with thinner areas and denser patches hanging on for dear

At the end of our his-and-her buzzing session, SecondBorn got the wig and I got the multicolored false eyelashes.

life. My head looked like a spotted dog and it hurt. Not intense pain, but wherever hair was left, if it touched anything, like my pillow or a hat, it felt prickly. It was a yucky feeling, like what you get from fingernails on a chalkboard.

I was semibald when I returned home with the boys. By the time my Chicago sister-in-law came for my next round of chemo, I'd had enough of the aching-scalp syndrome. Chicago lathered me up and shaved the stubborn patches off. I gotta tell ya, I was uuuggly. I don't care what lies my loved ones said. My head is about as white as snow, and it ain't pretty.

Contrary to popular belief, I did own and wear a variety of "normal" hats. I dressed up only for treatments. Here I am at Nursey's celebrating my 37th birthday.

FirstBorn and his friend expressed their reactions honestly. Both had seen my patchy G.I. Jane look. Neither had seen me bald. I was in my room wearing a hat. They were running in and out. I got a major tropical flash and yanked the hat off without thinking. Moments later the eleven-year-old neighbor entered, looked at me, screamed in horror, "Eeew!" covered his face, and bolted out of the room.

Intrigued, FirstBorn came and looked. He jumped back, waved his hands in front of his face, yelled, "Gross!" raced out the door, and shut it to protect himself from my monstrous appearance. Talk about your ego booster. I briefly thought about crying. Instead I concluded their heartfelt reactions were actually kind of funny. They both knew I was going bald and had seen me with less and less hair. What did they expect? I still laugh when I picture their facial expressions as they caught their first glimpse of my neon-white cue ball.

Everything I could make fun, I did. My trip to the wig store was no exception. I went before my hair fell out. I tried on everything from purple punk to blond bombshell to Afros. The more ridiculous the wig, the sillier it appeared, the more fun it was. I settled on something more subdued. At that point, I'd never dyed my hair, but always considered trying auburn. I figured being bald was the perfect opportunity. I picked a stylish shoulder-length auburn wig. It looked natural and attractive.

I ordered the smallest size they made. It was way too big. I have a very tiny head. The woman at the shop spent over an hour custom fitting it on my pinhead. There is only one picture of me in my wig. It was taken in the wig store.

My skin is very sensitive. I have a list of fabrics and products I can't use because I break out in rashes. I was hypersensitive during chemo. Guess what happened with the wig? I wore it out to dinner. The few hours I wore it, I was ready to crawl out of my skin. I couldn't wait to get that blinking rug off. I spent more time wig shopping and fitting it than the entire time I wore that itchy attachment. I donated it to an organization that provided low-income cancer patients with wigs.

Without a wig, I implemented Plan B: hats. I had already purchased a sleeping hat. The saleswoman told me it was a must, and boy was she right. People loose most of their heat through their head. Being bald is mighty cold when you're accustomed to long hair. Drafts are everywhere. Once wigless, I got a bunch of hats and caps in a variety of colors, fabrics, and styles. Some were gifts; some I bought. I matched the hats to my outfits. It was usually obvious I was bald underneath, but I chose not to let that bother me. After all, it was only for a short period of time.

People stare at bald women. It is natural to observe anything that's odd or different. We all do it. Not out of callousness or meanness, but curiosity or confusion. I remember a young boy standing behind me in the grocery store. He said, quite loudly, as children do, "I think she's bald under there." The mother was mortified.

I turned around, squatted to his level, and smiled. "You're right. I'm very sick, and the medicine made my hair fall out."

The boy was wide-eyed and moved his hand toward my head. I asked him, "Do you want to see?" He nodded and I pulled off my hat. He shrugged. He was much less shocked than my own son. I guess I didn't appear any different than the bald men he'd seen. Since I didn't make a big deal about being follically challenged, he didn't. Our perspective is often the gauge others use to determine how they should respond. Thankfully we have control over that gauge.

Being bald is an odd sensation for a woman. Men have it easy. Their shower and prep time is a breeze. When I went out, I put on makeup, but my eyelashes and eyebrows were thinning. By the end, I had about one lash every centimeter, which is better than none, but looked cartoonish.

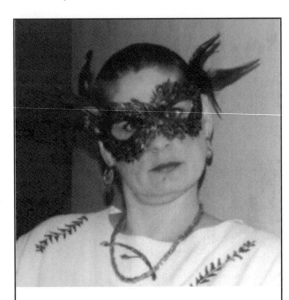

"What really scares me most, more than nukes or cancer, is a man or a woman without a sense of humor."—Jonathan Winters

I did have one added hygiene step. I had to oil my head. I didn't even know they made special polymers for naked scalps. Originally the demo lady said to apply two or three drops a day and massage it in. She dripped some on my head, and it disappeared. My skin was so dry I had to slather that stuff on. When it got colder, I had a humidifier pumping moisture into the air around the clock.

I greased the old noodle regularly. Not that the extra lubricant helped my thought process. I couldn't always connect words and sentences. It is difficult to describe what it felt like. I would start to......talk and there......would be..... long breaks......and pauses. Even on simple sentences. It was like talking to a robot with a short circuit. I would try to speak seamlessly. It's not like I'd ever had trouble talking in the past. I just couldn't. Talking was frustrating. It felt weird and spooky, like I was possessed. At times I could tell I was disconnecting, but my brain would remain in slow motion. Sometimes it stopped altogether. I'd have no idea what I was saying or where my mind was. I just knew it wasn't with the rest of my body.

And I pray that Christ will be more and more at home in your hearts, living with you as you trust in him. May your roots go down deep into the soil of God's marvelous love; and may you be able to feel and understand, as all God's children should, how long, how wide, how deep, and how high his love really is; and to experience this love for yourselves.

EPHESIANS 3:17-19A LAB

Chapter 8

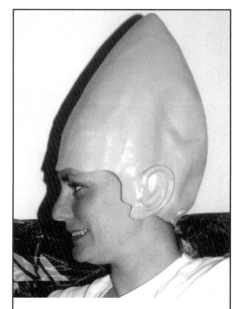

"Inviting people to laugh with you while you laugh at yourself is a good thing to do. You may be a fool, but you're the fool in charge." —Carl Reiner

By the fall of 1999, I just wanted the divorce done. I had filed for divorce in July of 1998. In theory, the entire process was supposed to take less than a year. Obviously, mine took longer. We ended up scheduled for a trial on September 14, 1999. I had completed my second round of chemo and would have my third treatment two days after the trial.

I was worried there would be another continuance. My attorney said cases over a year are not continued. I was skeptical. Dr. Drug 'Em Up wanted me to focus entirely on my health. The trial needed to happen as scheduled. This information was passed on to the judge. MouthPiece assured me my hardship request would be honored.

Days before the trial, Ex's attorney decided he needed to depose me. The only date available was the day before the trial. According to MouthPiece, the judge would be forced to grant a continuance if opposing counsel couldn't depose me. Dr. Drug 'Em Up wanted me to rest before the trial, but I was determined to get the divorce finalized. The deposition was supposed to take about an hour and I agreed to do it.

We started after lunch and didn't finish until dinnertime. In the deposition, I was asked questions about my siblings, gifts Ex's mother gave me, and other seemingly irrelevant topics. I asked my attorney what those questions had to do with the divorce. He called it a fishing expedition. The goal was to rattle me so I would appear irrational and unstable or would slip and say something damaging. Fortunately I had nothing to hide.

Pale, bald, and nauseated, I was deposed for four hours. As the questions continued, I grew feebler. I couldn't remember numbers or details. I felt exhausted and worn down. During a potty break, the court reporter came over to me, patted my hand, and told me I was doing a good job.

BigBrother and Mom drove in from out of town and met me at the lawyer's office. I had given BigBrother power of attorney. After dinner, I asked him to negotiate as he saw fit. I stayed a while, but was too wiped out to understand what was being discussed and went home.

I went to bed numb. The next morning I felt I was at death's door. I intended to drive myself to the courthouse. I was doing so poorly BigBrother drove me. I was crying and babbling incoherently. I was worried about my boys, my finances, and my health insurance. I was in no position to get a job, had no income, and still wanted to publish my novel.

BigBrother told me not to worry. No matter what the judge decided, he would help me. His only instructions after seeing me the previous twenty-four hours were, "Get it done today." We entered the courthouse single-minded: get the divorce behind me.

The witnesses were there and we were ready to go, yet somehow we never got started. Four of us were waiting in a small conference room. Then Ex's lawyer requested that the attorneys speak to the judge in chambers. My kid's counselor, BigBrother, and I all instructed MouthPiece, no matter what, don't let this be continued. He seemed confident, given my medical hardship plea and the age of the case, that we would proceed after a short delay.

Within an hour, despite our begging, we were heading home. Another continuance was granted. To this day I would like to know what the heck was said in those chambers. The only explanation given was Ex's attorney was unable to prepare after yesterday's deposition.

When I felt attacked from all sides, God had me start a one-woman attitude adjustment crusade. Humor was His weapon of choice. I was instructed to fight fearlessly against pessimistic self-talk and terminate the negative CDs playing in my head. I discovered the Holy Grail for happiness was consciously counting my blessings and focusing on the positives. My best protection against depression and hopelessness was to kill evil negative thoughts. I put on the armor of God, charged forth and conquered what was in my head. I took my destructive ideas and made them prisoners of war. My battlefield for happiness was in the mind, so that's where I needed to win the war.

Before we left the courthouse, just to get it over with, we accepted Ex's settlement offer on all the assets. He refused. We were willing to have the judge decide on the children's issues only. He refused. We were willing to settle any part that day. He refused. I was completely dangnified.

Two days later, I arrived at my oncologist's office for another fun-filled adventure in chemotherapy. Dr. Drug 'Em Up asked me how my divorce turned out. I told him the sordid details that accomplished nothing. We discussed my situation. I was getting more and more rundown as the treatments progressed and had months to go. Plus I had difficulty focusing my thoughts for any period of time.

Immediately after my third chemo treatment, there was another huge legal upheaval. Because the trial had been postponed, Ex and I had not gotten legally divorced. No divorce papers created a dilemma for Ex. He called and insisted I cosign for the duplex he was purchasing. My brain may have been crashing, but it wasn't completely offline. I had handled mortgage loans when I was in banking. I knew lenders required legally married spouses to both sign the loan papers. I was also familiar with the potential problems that could arise if I did sign.

There were tons of phone calls between Ex, BigBrother, myself, and the attorneys. It was discouraging to throw more money down the legal black hole. MouthPiece agreed it was a bad idea for me to sign. Well, duh. On the other hand, I didn't want to prevent Ex from purchasing his duplex. It was a good choice for him and the boys. I didn't know what to do.

Chemo left me sick and drained. I felt weak, helpless, and attacked. I wanted a hero who would jump in and save the day — a buff warrior who would fight my battles for me. I looked to my Savior, who guided me with some unique meditations.

During my divorce and treatments, I read Scripture before bed. The bookmark in my Bible was a greeting card. It had a painting of *The Lord is My Shepherd* by Warner Sallman. Every night, Jesus was in the valley, standing among the sheep, holding a lamb. The vision of a gentle, loving Christ was great when I needed to be held in the palm of His hand. When I was sick and knee-deep in conflict with Ex, the Good Shepherd image didn't cut it for me. I needed a defender who could break the strongholds in my life.

Enter Kung Fu Christ, a tailor-made image just for me. In my mind, I'd see Sallman's painting only I made modifications. The pasture was surrounded with stone barriers. Each stone was engraved with words that represented my pain and problems. Nausea. Weakness. Divorce. Depositions. Fear. Mortgages. The Sallman Good Shepherd would scan all my problems and nod. He would gently put down the lamb and remove his outer tunic. Underneath was a buff Savior with bulging muscles.

As Kung Fu Christ, He would karate chop, round kick, and head butt all my struggles. The stone barriers would crack and crumble under His mighty power. When all my obstacles had been destroyed, Kung Fu Christ would put His outer tunic back on, pick up the lamb, and become the Good Shepard again. I always felt better after my superhero Kung Fu Christ had saved the day. I had another equally ludicrous image.

I broke a few fundamental rules of dignity in this book. My approach to life and writing isn't exactly traditional. On the other hand, when you look at the word "fundamental," if you take out the "fun," what's left is "da mental," and I see too many people who live like that.

You have to hear the Rocky Theme Song in the background as I relay the dialogue going through my head. Let's get ready to rumble. In this corner, in red trunks, the serpent of evil, the lover of lies, Satan the Snake. (The crowd boos and hisses.) In this corner, wearing dazzling white, the Jehovah of Justice, the Lord of Love, Almighty Abba. (The crowd whistles and cheers.)

The competitors moved to the center of the ring. Satan the Snake throws a left filled with chemotherapy side effects followed by a right upper cut of divorce proceedings. Almighty Abba blocks them both. He body slams Satan the Snake. My fears and pain are given a massive rib crushing. My problems go down for the count under Almighty Abba's power. By the time I finished the Rocky Theme Song, I was usually smiling. Almighty Abba was my lean, mean attitude-adjusting machine; the one who could cut through my strongest mental mayhem.

These goofy fantasies can be blamed or credited (depending on your view) to my kids. I never gave karate or wrestling a second thought until my boys ran around playing them constantly. The image of a Kung Fu Christ or an Almighty Abba isn't sacrilegious. It is an example of how far our loving Father will go to reassure and heal us. If our motives are pure and we are truly seeking Him, our God will go to any lengths to reach us. It makes sense that He would use ideas and images that we can relate to and remember.

Jesus was willing to be publicly humiliated to save us. He wants to be our Savior, our lover, and our friend. I used to be so hung up on the legalism that I couldn't have fun with Christ. Good friends are silly and laugh together. You may think I'm crazy. I babble with God constantly, poor fellow. I include Him in every aspect of my life. I know plenty of Christians who praise God for their blessings, seek His guidance in their lives, and His comfort in their pain, but do not include God in their recreation. We are not supposed to compartmentalize our time with God. Our Father wants to share our fun. What parent wouldn't? Invite Him to join you when you play.

I have gotten much better with this. I spend lots of time alone. When I need a companion, Jesus is always there. We read comic books together, eat together, walk together, and watch movies together. I don't need an imaginary friend because I share my life with the Living God.

I prayed for Kung Fu Christ and Almighty Abba to resolve the duplex situation. God presented a solution I didn't even know existed. Ex and I ended up legally divorced without resolving any of the financial or parenting issues. It felt like the contradiction it is. I was divorced while still having the entire divorce process ahead of me. Oh well, it solved the immediate problem. All the mortgage company needed was a divorce decree from the court and the judge gave us that.

My first and third chemo treatments were the worst. The first was terrible because it felt like they gave me enough drugs to kill an elephant. The third was hard because I was exhausted from the deposition and canceled trial before I received treatment. Then immediately after, I dealt with the duplex issue and getting legally divorced instead of resting and recovering. It was horrible. I didn't have the mental capacity or the emotional reserve to handle both chemo and the divorce proceedings. I was a mess.

I spoke with Dr. Drug 'Em Up. Together we came to the conclusion that the legal process had to stop until I was well. In his opinion I was in no condition to make important decisions. (Not being able to complete sentences will give people that impression.) Grudgingly I asked the court to postpone settling the issues. My doctor wrote a letter to the judge stating, for medical reasons, everything needed to be postponed until I recovered from treatment. Asking for an indefinite continuance was discouraging. I thought my divorce would never, ever end. Having the legal divorce decree was a formality that changed nothing.

I would not be able to resume the "divorce" proceedings until January 2000. We settled the issues in May 2000. It took almost another year to be done. In the end I had one final hearing. There the judge ordered Ex to finish the transfer paperwork for the retirement benefits. The last details were finally completed in the spring of 2001.

There were many days when I couldn't keep up with the rest of the herd.

Dismiss all anxiety from your minds. Present your needs to God in every form of prayer and in petitions full of gratitude. Then God's own peace, which is beyond all understanding, will stand guard over your hearts and minds in Christ Jesus.

PHILIPPIANS 4:6-7 NA

Chapter 9

After I received my final divorce decree, I asked friends if they knew any men who wanted to date a bald chick. Sadly, I found no single men with a bald fetish. So poor little Scarlet NoHaira was forced to wait to reenter the dating scene. When I finished treatment and had grown a respectable amount of hair, I began dating. I think I'd rather face chemotherapy again.

"Normal is in the eye of the beholder."
—Whoppi Goldberg

I originally thought I would not encumber my dating experience by setting unrealistic standards. I would give everyone a chance. Shortly after, I got to know a man from church. He was significantly older, a theme I've found throughout dating. It seems men only want to date much younger women. The man bagged groceries at the supermarket. He was illiterate. He came to the church office for help. I wrote addresses on his envelopes for mailing. He asked me out. I decided to set at least a minimum standard for dating: the men had to be literate.

I joined a Catholic singles Bible study in a large affluent church. I assumed the potential would be greater in that environment. Wrong. I met another older gentleman there. He offered, unsolicited, the following information: He lives in a small rural community on several acres. He mows his grass in a loincloth. He does not believe in banks and has no checking account. He doesn't use natural gas and rarely uses electricity. He cuts his own firewood and kills or grows his own food. He also states, without prompting, because no one would ask such a thing, he doesn't use toilet paper; he uses cornhusks. I have sensitive skin and only use premium TP brands. He invited me to his farm for a home-caught and cooked meal. I kindly declined and decided I need a new dating standard: the men must be literate and must use toilet paper.

The first time I met another semi-attractive man, he described in detail how he stole motorcycles. He was apparently good at stealing, because he'd never been caught. He told me at the end of our casual dinner I was "cute enough" to call again. OK, so I needed a new, new standard: the men must be literate, must use toilet paper, and must be law abiding.

Not too long after that, I met another diamond in the rough. This man spent over an hour describing his LSD trips. How he thought he was flying, how he nearly jumped out a window, and how he thought his hand was on fire. This news may surprise you, but I didn't ask how to steal motorcycles or what acid-induced hallucinations were like. Yet similar to the thief above, the druggie chose to reveal this information the first time we met. Those were their put-your-best-foot-forward topics of conversation. Can you imagine what they could be hiding? Time to set a new, new, new standard: no illiterates, no TP substitutes, no grand larceny, and no illegal drug use.

I briefly tried an online Christian dating service. A man from India began e-mailing me. Logistics aside, he stated he was a Catholic priest. Obviously he was not too knowledgeable about Catholicism, because he didn't realize priests took vows of celibacy. Time for a new, new, new, new standard: no illiteracy, no cornhusks, no outstanding warrants, no illegal drug use, and no broken vows, real or fabricated.

Sigh, poor little Scarlet NoHaira is still single. I know it's because I'm way too picky. Do I get discouraged about dating? Of course, look at what I'm up against. How do I handle it? Sometimes I feel depressed and cry. I also laugh at myself and my unique dating experiences. I gripe to friends and I pray.

Fiddle-dee-dee, I'm still a single she.

I actually have been out with normal men. Our values often clash. The second time I went out with one gentleman, he asked to see my bedroom. Hint. Hint. I politely declined and he never called again. Rejection is painful, no matter what the reason.

At Thanksgiving I was poultry in motion. Only God knows when our goose is going to be cooked. Time in prayer is the bread and butter of a happy life. Be thankful for your family and friends. Gobble up time with the people you love. Healthy relationships are with people who mix encouragement into our hopes and dreams. They are interested in our feelings, activities, and needs. A "full"filling relationship is like the smell of a fresh-baked apple pie. Its sweet aroma permeates the rooms of our hearts and reminds us of Christ's love. Healthy people provide us with a cornucopia of joy, support, assistance, and fun.

On the other hand, the devil's lies make us sicker than spoiled meat. He grinds our insecurities and weaknesses into self-doubting dishes. When you swallow his manipulative mush, he stuffs you with sorrow. His promises never provide nourishment. His in"greed"ients include hate, lust, anger, bitterness, and rebellion. Satan's soup is filled with sin and should be spit out. The devil is a master chef at spooning out pain.

Take Satan's stew off your menu and order fun-filled time with your family and friends instead. Be a glutton for quality time with them because they are the gravy of life. When you baste your days with loving people, good things cook up.

My lack of success in dating is hard on my self-esteem. I have been single ten years. I've been on dozens of dates, but haven't dated anyone special. My relational failures can feel insurmountable. It's so easy to play the what's-wrong-with-me game. Everyone has emotional triggers, but all joy-robbers have certain similarities. Some are more intense than others. Emotionally charged situations are enemies of a peaceful mental state. Negative emotions feed our insecurities. They can steal our peace and joy in minutes.

Some days the devil is relentless. His voice echoes in stereo from every corner of my mind that I am not lovable as I am. When the pain and vulnerability levels are high, we are powerless without faith. Satan always attacks our weaknesses. When I'm not at peace, I know I'm not in Christ. Any thoughts that put me in contact with my emotional triggers destroy my present state of mind. I can't pray traditional prayers. Just saying certain words even in prayer, can detonate pain and sadness bombs. I have to purge the entire thought process from my brain. That's why I use meditation.

I get in bed with my electric blanket. I visualize myself held closely in the palm of God's hand. As I inhale I say, "Your peace in." I exhale saying, "Obsessive thinking out." "Obsessive thinking" is the catchall for anything I can't get off my mind. It allows me to avoid the trigger words themselves. When a trigger pops into my consciousness, I don't get upset. I repeat my phrase and go on. On a mediocre day, ten minutes of meditation gets me back on track, on bad days it takes forty-five.

I use this for everything I obsess about, from kids, to money, to relationships, to bad days. The general mantra keeps me from any specific fixations. Like all skills, as I've practiced, I've improved. I can usually reestablish Christ's peace without too much trouble. If I have to, I can meditate in the car, in line, at work, or anywhere else.

Now I struggle with the relationship issues more than other areas. The holes in my heart are too big to let my mind get started. If I don't refocus my thoughts immediately, I give the devil a foothold. He can quickly make me feel rejected and unloved. In my vulnerable areas, I pray the Holy Spirit destroys both the known and unknown triggers in my mind.

It probably comes as no surprise to you that I can relate to Dr. Seuss's humor. My boys and I always loved his books. When the boys were little, I had numerous books memorized. My poem is a tribute to his classic works.

J. CATS IN HER HATS

My boy looked and he saw me in a spiked wig.
Later I wore antlers and the nose of a pig.
A turkey head, a conehead, well that's something new.
A Viking hat, A Bug's Life, and a Teletubby I'll do.

When he saw me leaving the house in each hat,
My boy, he said, "Why do you step out there like that?
I know you are sick, and chemo is bad,
But you're looking so weird, and that's really sad."

I answered him plainly, as best as I could
As I stood there wearing my Arabian hood.
"I know it is strange. Don't you worry my son,
I'm making those horrible treatment trips fun.

"I have these two growths, Growth Two and Growth One.
It's cancer, you see, and can't be outrun.
I've had surgery, I'm sick, and I'm tired, that's true,
But I won't let it turn my attitude blue.

"My thoughts and reactions I can control.
I will not descend in a negative hole.
Cancer has hurt me, but I'll laugh my way through.
I won't let it destroy my happiness too.

"I'll laugh and be silly, up through the end.
This dreadful disease I will transcend.
And when I am cured, you'll look back and you'll see,
My hats and my wigs were a diversion for me."

I spent too many years praying while Satan screamed in my ear. I have to silence the devil's voice to clearly hear God's. I was, and sometimes still am, a prisoner of my own mind. Don't make the same mistake. Fight back. Your mental attitude may or may not change your outcome, but it can drastically change the quality of your life. It is the peace beyond all understanding Scripture promises.

I've known physically healthy Christians emotionally suffering to death. Year upon year they are miserable. If just this or just that would happen, they would be happy. On the other hand, I've known terminally ill people who accepted their situations and kept on living. You can be alive on the outside and totally dead on the inside.

If I waited for the perfect marriage, financial security, and a successful career, I might never be happy. I've made a conscious choice to thank God for the blessings in my current situation. I can either focus on being alone and dateless or be thrilled with the extra writing time. I can be discouraged I'm not a successful author or remember how much I love writing. I can be stressed by my job or be thankful that I have a job and health insurance. I can complain about all the wants I can't afford or be grateful for all the needs I can.

My life isn't perfect. I'll bet yours isn't either. Life is hard. Some people are more blessed than others, but we're all stuck with unfairness and imperfection. Don't let those stop you from being happy. You can either learn to appreciate what you have, or be miserable about what you don't. It is your choice.

Abraham Lincoln said it best, "Most folks are about as happy as they make up their minds to be." Make up your mind to be happy today, right now. If you wait until life is fair and trouble-free, you may die waiting, and I guarantee that you'll be dying while you wait.

✳✳✳

My fourth and final chemo treatment was the easiest. SisterTwo came and helped. I cannot remember one tidbit about her visit. My level of exhaustion was so great I slept most of the time. By November of 1999 I was finished with chemo. Whew!

It was time to start annoying Dr. Burn 'Em Up and his radiation crew. Some people need radiation before surgery or chemo. For me it was the last stand. Everyone's radiation experience is different. Just like there are different types of chemo, there are different ways to do radiation. The common denominator for radiation is to lock phasers on target and fry the cancerous tissue.

Given my horrendous experience with chemo, Dr. Burn 'Em Up was not hopeful I'd do well in radiation. I had a bunch of factors "stacked" against me. The biggest was my breast had already been subjected to major surgery and my body to chemo. Also against me was my sensitive, fair skin. Plus the cancer had been on the left underside of my breast. That meant radiation would be concentrated in an area that wasn't easy to keep cool or aired. I anticipated more time topless, arms over head, and reclined.

I was being nuked in the cold of winter, so I was faced with another potential temperature dilemma. How to keep warm without anything heavy or itchy near sore, burned skin. Mom decided the solution was my grandmother's old mink coat. It was warm, lightweight, and soft inside and out. Mom's theory was I could run around the house topless under the fur coat. I imagined myself wandering, and I do mean wandering, around the house, weak from treatment, topless, in sweatpants, socks, fuzzy slippers, and a mink coat. When I pictured myself wearing such a classy outfit, I had to laugh.

I didn't end up donning that particular costume. Compared to chemotherapy, I aced radiation. I was well enough to drive myself to all thirty-three treatments. I was tired and weak, but I didn't burn badly. I was sore, and my chest was sensitive, but I wasn't miserable. Many people get second-and-third degree burns. I had something similar to a bad sunburn. I also had no time to feel sorry for myself or focus on the discomfort. Unlike chemo, where I had three weeks in between treatments, I had radiation five days a week. It was tough, in my semilucid state, to devise a new outfit and goofy retort every day. Each day's creation consumed much of my waking moments.

The prep for radiation treatment is different for everyone. I had more topless measurements and markings. In addition to the pen markings, Dr. Burn 'Em Up wanted me permanently tagged in case the cancer returned.

That's medical jargon for, "We're going to tattoo you." I didn't have to go downtown to some seedy parlor either. I was tattooed in the doctor's office by a highly trained technician. I have four small circular marks around my chest. Good thing tattoos are popular these days. Instead of telling people I was branded for cancer treatment, I enthusiastically stated I had gotten some tattoos: a period, an eight ball, a dot, and the pupil of an eye.

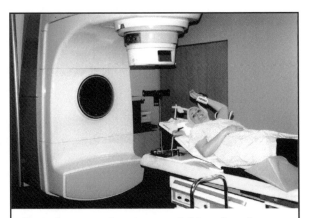

"Laughter can be more satisfying than honor; more precious than money; more heart-cleansing than prayer." —Harriet Rochlin

For the duration of my radiation treatments, I went Monday through Friday. Generally, each individual is assigned a time and goes at that time every day. I was a

10:30 person. After waving at the receptionist, I'd go straight to a dressing room and undress from the waist up. I would keep my hat or costume on while I sat in my airy hospital gown along the waiting wall. When it was my turn in the tanning booth, I was hooked up and my dots aligned. The treatments only took five to ten minutes. I felt almost nothing, kind of like radiation from the sun. You don't feel yourself being burned, but the results are evident later.

Although radiation was significantly easier for me than chemo, it did make me extremely tired. It was tedious going every day. On the low days, I called upon my motto, "Dignity, always maintain dignity." There are those who might say my motto was an oxymoron to my behavior. I'd like to give you a different perspective. Which is more dignified: suffering in silence or making the best of a terrible situation? Remember we affect the others around us.

For the most part, during radiation I waited with the same cancer patients. I'd see the 10:15, 10:30, and 10:45 people. One day an older gentleman was unexpectedly there. Gramps was in his eighties and alone. His wife had died, and his children lived out of state. He must have had some sort of skin or facial cancer. On his face were the white and blue markings for the radiation tech. His face was blistered and oozing from the treatments. I held his hand. I don't remember what ridiculous outfit I was wearing, but he laughed, be it with me or at me. He told me his regular time was in the afternoon. That day he had come early so he could see another doctor later.

The next week Gramps was there at 10:30 a number of days. I asked him why. He told me he could no longer go out because his face was so hideous. He was alone and discouraged. He added with tears in his eyes, "I changed my time because you're the only thing I have to look forward to each day."

I was on cloud nine. I cannot imagine anything more dignified than that. I'm convinced one of the keys to happiness is giving to others. It's a paradox: the more we give and care about others, the more we receive and others care about us. Selfishness is a direct path to unhappiness.

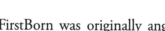

FirstBorn was originally angry, almost enraged, at what he viewed as my flippant attitude toward a life-threatening illness. He thought I was taking unnecessary risks with my life. Like so many of us, FirstBorn assumed acting serious was synonymous with taking life seriously. In fact, the two are very different. I had two young boys who needed a mother. In no way was I playing Russian roulette with my future. I diligently followed through on every recommendation my doctors made, like forcing myself to eat when I had mouth sores.

"To be playful and serious at the same time is possible, and it defines the ideal mental condition." —John Dewey

Once I convinced FirstBorn that acting serious was not the same as taking my health seriously, he whole-heartily supported my goofy diversions. He became my ten-year-old personal photographer. As my own junior paparazzi, FirstBorn snapped almost every picture in this book. They aren't perfect. We were taking pictures for fun. Sometimes perfection is overrated. If we eliminated everything that isn't perfect, we'd discard much of what makes life meaningful.

SecondBorn immediately embraced silliness as a way of life. I guess he didn't fall far from the tree. He also took a few pictures. Both kids made suggestions for costumes and comments. Many I used. Some were stranger than even I was willing to do, which is saying a lot.

If you love only those who love you, what good is that? Even scoundrels do that much. If you are friendly only to your friends, how are you different from anyone else? Even the heathens do that.

MATTHEW 5:46-47 LAB

Chapter 10

Ex wanted the boys for Christmas the first year we were separated and I agreed. It was a painful holiday. I didn't see my kids on Christmas Eve or Christmas Day. The following year when Mom came for the canceled divorce trial, she invited me to bring the boys to her place for Christmas. The vindictive part of me wanted Ex to experience the pain and loneliness I had the previous year. The kids wanted to see both parents on Christmas Eve and Christmas Day. I planned to give them what they wanted.

Intellectually it was easy to come to that conclusion. Sadly, it was a lot harder for me to act that noble. After two months of prayer and counseling, I finally sent Ex an e-mail about Christmas. I was trying to be nice. I quote my December 6, 1999 note verbatim, errors and all:

"The boys would like to see you on Christmas Eve and Christmas Day. I assume you will want to do that. If you want to see them on Christmas Eve. They need to be back here by 4:30, so I can do dinner, etc. I am planning on going to 10:30 AM Mass on Christmas morning. Then, if you'd like, they can go to your house for the afternoon and I can pick them up by 5:00 for dinner."

Ex replied it was not legally my year for Christmas because all issues had been left pending by the court. That meant there was no written agreement for the holidays. Therefore, he wanted the boys for Christmas Eve, Christmas morning, and Christmas dinner. I could have them on Christmas Eve from 2:30 to 7:00 and Christmas Day from 10:30 to 6:00.

All I want for Christmas are my locks of hair,
My locks of hair, my locks of hair.
All I want for Christmas are my locks of hair,
Then I could wish you Hairy Christmas.

I remember two times when I felt kicked in the gut: when I found out I had invasive cancer, and the Christmas incident. I was tired of struggles and conflicts. I kept trying to avoid them. When I received Ex's response, I completely lost it. I called Mom sobbing so hard she could not tell which daughter was on the phone. When she figured out it was me, she assumed I had life-and-death cancer news. I was so upset I couldn't tell her any different. I just bawled and did that erratic hysterical breathing that comes with intense crying. Once I calmed down, Mom helped me realize this was not the end of the world.

A combination of things made fighting over holiday time more difficult than other challenges. It was Christmas. I'd already had six long months of treatment. I still had to go to radiation every day. I was physically run down, emotionally

When walking the tightrope of life, the best balance is an eternal perspective. It's a three-ring circus out there. Dozens of things are pushing and shoving to take their place as our Big Top priority. Only God should have that spot.

To be a star performer on this stage of life, we must trust God with our anxieties. It seems easy by ourselves when we're only juggling a few small emotional balls, but when we're forced to play with fire, without Jesus we're going to get burned. Prayer is like a flame retardant suit; it protects us when we jump through life's fiery hoops.

Try not to monkey around with issues and problems the size of trained fleas. Ask yourself will it matter tomorrow? In a month? In a year? If the answers are no, that's your ticket out of the house of mirrors where little hang-ups are distorted into big problems.

The evil villain, Satan, will use kernels of delusion popped in our own fears and insecurities to convince us of his lies. His acts include confusion, fear, and guilt. The devil floats manipulation balloons filled with hot air, empty promises, and sleight-of-hand tricks. He shoots cannons full doubt into our hopes and dreams.

He is a ringmaster at shoving us back into the house of mirrors. He will distort any situation to keep us from Christ's love. Crack the faith whip at the devil's deeds and don't let him clown around with your happiness.

drained, and my finances were tight. It hurt most of all because it had taken a great deal of personal growth for me to offer Ex time on Christmas Eve and Christmas Day.

From an eternal perspective, a conflict over Christmas is not a big deal. At the time, it just felt overwhelming. I meditated and cried. I called on Coach Christ, Almighty Abba, Kung Fu Christ, and every other power image I could think of, and still I cried. I went to Mass, came home, and cried. I was exhausted and hurt. I cried more that week than the week I was diagnosed. My brain immediately understood this was not a life-altering situation, but it took over a week to calm my feelings down.

OK, so initially I failed that perspective test. The question is not whether we fall down. The question is, do we get back up? Do we continue to trust God when we feel hopeless and discouraged? How do we respond when we did what was right and still got burned?

Sometimes it was difficult to know when I should and shouldn't reply to Ex. The Christmas incident was an example. I was so dangnified. I wanted to say quite a few things to Ex. From the time we separated, my counselor suggested Ex and I correspond via e-mail. E-mail prevented me from lashing out and making unproductive comments. At that point in my life, I did not possess the self-control to verbally stop from snapping back. My commitment to e-mail allowed me to cool off and phrase things as neutrally as possible.

I typed a firm, but not scathing e-mail to Ex. Then I employed a tactic that had worked before. I didn't send the note. I prayed for God's will about the note and what to do. I asked God to honor my desire to do His will, not my flawed human ability to hear it and do it. God is obviously in cahoots with my computer.

After praying, I instructed my computer to send my e-mails. POOF, the letter to Ex disappeared. It hadn't been sent. It was completely gone! Missing in action. My other messages were sent without incident, but the message to Ex got "lost."

God's answer was clear. No additional comments. I'd gotten that response before. In fact, not once, not twice, but three times during my divorce, after praying, only the e-mails to Ex disappeared. God is in control of everything, including cyberspace.

I restated my original offer to no avail. I hated chucking more money at my attorney, but felt I had to pass the problem off to MouthPiece. He assured me it did not matter what was in writing. If Ex had the kids last year for Christmas, they should be with me this year.

The games went on for two weeks before Ex accepted my original offer. In the midst of the emotional upheaval, I dragged myself to radiation every day. My squirrelly hats and wigs were probably what kept me sane. You might question the sane part, but I must note, I never got committed.

The boys and I had a good Christmas. We had plenty to be thankful for. My absolute final, hopefully never again to be repeated treatment, was on December 22, 1999. As I completed my adventures with cancer, it seemed apropos we were ushering in a new millennium. I was ready to put numerous things in my past, but hope to retain the lessons I learned for a lifetime.

I learned I had to be the person I wanted to be each day, with these problems and this ex-husband, not tomorrow with easier issues or other people. I am only responsible for my motives, thoughts, and actions. We cannot stop ourselves from being hurt, but we can and are required to control our responses.

It's not a challenge to be kind and considerate when life is easy and others are treating us fairly. True character is revealed in how we respond when we absolutely do not feel like it or when we think the other person doesn't deserve it. Not that I was perfect or ever will be. Ex's version of the divorce would be substantially different.

All I can do is make a conscious effort not to react out of frustration, pain, and anger today, right now. It does not come naturally for me or anyone else. I know when I'm being selfish and when my motives aren't pure, and so does God. I constantly pray that Christ changes my actions, thoughts, and heart.

God wants to change us from the inside out because our thoughts and emotions determine our actions. It's like the old computer saying GIGO, which stands for Garbage In Garbage Out. If you put garbage in your mind in the form of negative thoughts, anger and frustration, don't be surprised when that's all your brain spits out. The devil loves GIGO. To get us out of Christ's peace, all Satan has to do is bombard our minds with negative messages. He gets our minds fixed in that annoying playback mode. Our thoughts repeat unpleasant or unresolved conflicts over and over. We fantasize about what we could or should have said or done.

When my thoughts are on repeat, I consciously try to put in a new CD. Prayer and meditation are great refocusing CDs, if and only if, I don't think about the issue I'm trying to purge from my thoughts. Otherwise, I'm just playing the same old CD on a different track. It's not that God doesn't hear those prayers. It's just that the devil is often yelling the entire time I'm praying.

Counting my blessings also helps. Music, walking, exercising, playing with the kids, gardening, a bubble bath, anything that helps me refocus is good. I often use humor as a replacement CD. I watch funny movies or TV shows, read humor or comic books, or laugh with family and friends.

Humor and fun are not replacements for time with our Lord. They are additional weapons in our arsenal against destructive thoughts. A good laugh lightens our mood, but for humor to be an effective secret weapon, God must be doing the aiming.

If you're always missing your happiness target, look at who is aiming your weapon. A powerful weapon, incorrectly aimed, won't destroy its target and often causes collateral damage. Half destroyed targets rebuild and refortify and Satan loves to help in that process. It is only through faith that we can safely chart a course through our emotional minefields. God helps us defuse our pain, fear, and doubt bombs. If your army is losing, I encourage you to follow a different leader. Happiness is an inside job, but we're not meant to be an army of one. Let Jesus be the general of your life and I promise you'll be victorious.

We wish you a Hairy Christmas.
We wish you a Hairy Christmas.
We wish you a Hairy Christmas
And a healthy New Year.

Oncology patients are encouraged to visualize the cancer cells leaving their bodies and to even talk to their illness. I did both. Just as Moses tried to persuade Pharaoh to "Let my people go," I dressed as Mosezina, attempted to convince the cancer to "Let my body go!" I felt called to drive the cancer out of my body using humor and a positive attitude.

I warned my nasty, sinful cancer cells of the plagues I would rain down upon it. I began with my first surgery: the slice-and-dice plague. It did not deter my evil enslaver. I warned them before my second surgery, "Let my body go, or I shall cut you to pieces." Those hard-hearted tormentors refused to release my body. When my lymph nodes were clear, I thought those rapidly dividing little devils were finally listening and I would soon be free of the bondage.

I gave those stubborn cells every opportunity to release me. I warned them of the horrors of chemo. "Let my body go, or I shall call a poison down upon you. You shall crawl on your belly and your tissue shall rot." (Hey, I was desperate and I knew one of us was going to be crawling on their belly.) Those deceitful devils were undeterred. I was forced to raise my IV pole to the heavens and call the chemo curse down upon those crafty cancer cells.

My body continued to be rebellious. I climbed Mt. Sigh-I and received Mosezina's Ten Chemo Commandments. I was instructed to give the Is-Real life cancer clan the sacred laws listed below.

As for me and my body, the obstinate cancer devils refused to free me. I warned those hard-hearted souls of radiation, "Let my body go, or I shall burn you in a fiery furnace." They refused to listen. I was forced to subject them to the final plague. Yet good would prevail. The week of Christmas 1999, I parted the white-coated sea of medical personnel and crossed over into the promised land of cancer-free.

Mosezina's Ten Commandments

1. Thou shall not get stuck with any more needles.

2. Thou shall not worship the porcelain altar.

3. Thou shall not take the name of doctors in vain.

4. Thou shall not eat unclean hospital food.

5. Thou shall not covet thy neighbor's health.

6. Thou shall not independently support drug and insurance companies.

7. Thou shall have a positive attitude.

8. Thou shall celebrate life.

9. Thou shall love and appreciate your family and friends.

10. Thou shall get well soon.

We also rejoice in our sufferings, because we know that suffering produces perseverance; perseverance, character; and character, hope.

ROMANS 5:3B-4 NIV

Chapter 11

This dumb bunny finally nabbed some hair.

While the fur was flying over the Christmas schedule, the boys convinced me to go window shopping at a local pet store. Never, ever go into a pet store with your children when you're feeling weak. It is a four-legged disaster waiting to happen.

FirstBorn's pet rat (don't even ask how I got talked into that) had recently died. When you're low, those fuzzy critters seem so lovable. The pet salesman was extremely helpful. He offered to let us hold a few baby rabbits. It doesn't take a rocket scientist to guess what happened. The boys were quick to remind me we had an empty rat cage at home. The kids and the salesman convinced me a pet rabbit would be an easy, low-maintenance pet. Yeah, right.

When we let the bunny out, he was supposed to roam free only in the kitchen. For months, no barrier was too high, too strong, or too secure to hold our pet. BunBun managed to chew through, jump over, move, or tear down any obstacle in his path. It became a battle of wills, and the bunny was winning. Finding a way to corral the critter became a matter of personal pride. I guess I wanted to feel like I was beating something. I was not going to be outsmarted by a blinking rabbit.

After six or seven failed attempts, our final barrier required a five-foot by three-foot piece of heavy particleboard; a gate made of PVC pipe, chicken wire, and duct tape; two chairs; and a six-pack of soda. When the bunny was out of his cage, to enter the kitchen, we had to step up on one chair, over the board, onto the other chair, and back down to the floor. Doesn't that sound "low maintenance" and "easy" to set up and work around?

BunBun was not my best pet decision, a bigger mistake than the rat, which is saying a lot. After a year and a half, I got tired of climbing over the barrier. BunBun was also biting and having accidents in the house. I finally put the rabbit out of my misery. SecondBorn is still mad I sent BunBun hopping off to bunny heaven.

I personally love furry critters. They add a great deal to our lives and can reflect God's unconditional love. Pets don't care what we look like, how popular we are, or how much money we have.

When we became petless, the boys wanted a puppy. I didn't feel ready. After treatment, it took me a long time to regain my energy level. Not one to repeat my mistakes, this time I went pet shopping alone. I found a kitten at the local shelter. Fluffball was a playful cuddly hit. As an adult cat, she is the queen. She believes we humans are blessed to serve her. She is my typing companion. She is often perched on my shoulder purring as I work. When my typing gets in the way of a serious catnap, Fluffball curls up on the file cabinet or a chair in the corner.

As a single woman I'm often home alone. I began to consider a dog for protection. I had no intention of adding a puppy to my workload. In 2002, a fully trained lab/chow mix needed a good home. I jumped at the chance. Everyone was thrilled except the cat.

When the dog arrived, Fluffball was quite vocal with her disdain. Poochy quietly crawled toward the cat on his four paws, but regardless of his humble approach, she wanted no part of the pooch. She quickly became our invisible cat. I let her front claws grow. I figured one good smack and the dog would stay away. Violence was beneath her dignity. Fluffball has never scratched anyone.

I removed her bell so the dog couldn't hear her coming. As stealth-kitty, she darted from one safe vantage point to another. Poochy never did anything remotely aggressive. It seemed the potential threat was unsettling. They have learned to coexist. Poochy wants to play and Fluffball remains aloof. I feel much safer having a big dog around. The kids and I love him and he is my walking buddy.

By the end of treatment I was physically wiped out. The doctor said it would take two to three years to fully recover. It took my body about that long. Some of the simple things, like adding pets, made me feel my life was back to normal. Exercise was another.

Reintroducing exercise was an uphill battle. About eighteen months after treatment, I decided to try "jogging." It's in quotes because I started by going down my short driveway and all the way across the street. At the time, that little exertion was extremely difficult. For moral support, I would ask one of the boys to go with me. Frankly, it took us longer to put on our shoes than we spent running. If they were watching TV, I had to wait for a commercial. Then they could go and return without missing anything. Ever the supportive sons, they still laugh about me hyperventilating at the end of those long, thirty-second workouts.

Her Royal Majesty, Queen Fluffball, will now present her State of the Kingdom address from The Flowered Throne Room.

The year of our Lord 2002 started out "purr"fectly wonderful. My three loyal subjects were properly tending to my every need. I waltzed freely and regally throughout the land ruling with a soft paw. Then a black cloud descended upon my sovereign realm: A hideous hound arrived. I was forced underground. I had to go hours without food or servants! I spied on the intruder for days. It became obvious this invader intended to stay. He brought two beds, a huge feed-and-water trough, toys, and smelly bones. I launched a fierce attack. I shuttered, I hissed, I growled at the beast. I did my best to expel the evil interloper. Unfortunately, he employed a cruel and despicable military tactic: obedience to humans.

He is black from head to toe, with beady dark eyes. Even his tongue is black; hence, I call him the Black Knight. This vile intruder has brought humiliation and shame to my kingdom. He has no respect for the human/pet hierarchy. He refuses to assume his rightful place and will take orders from my human servants. How he can hold his disgusting head up is beyond me. He is so demented he loves leather objects of torture called leashes. These devices are used by humans to lead animals around. The stupid oaf actually enjoys this indignity. I now have my paws full trying to retrain the peasants.

Alas, my efforts to force this vile monster out have failed. For my subject's sake, I have been forced to negotiate a tentative treaty. The Black Knight acknowledges my superior breeding and will crawl on his hands and knees before my throne. I would never deign to mingle with such a despicable creature; however, in the best interest of peace, I do allow him to grovel before me. He even had the audacity to enter my master bedroom where no dog had gone before. He has also stolen my most prized lookout, the back door. I must now rule and watch from high perches or by slinking under the furniture. Despite the horrors I'm enduring, I refuse to abdicate. I will continue to fight to reclaim my kingdom; but alas, I fear the Black Knight will be an ongoing menace.

The Black Knight gives her Royal Highness a bow-wow bow.

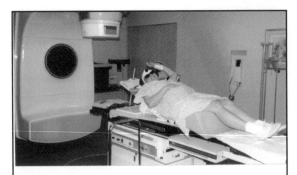

Have an *operation* on your *attitude*. Extract your negative thoughts and transplant them with positive ones.

It is another example of mind over matter. I could have focused on how little I was doing, or been hurt by their comments. Instead, I reminded myself what I was accomplishing and the example of perseverance I was setting. Slowly I was able to run to the neighbor's driveway, to the next street, for an entire block, a quarter of a mile, and so on. My endurance had been severely compromised. I had to fight to rebuild it. After a year of building up to a mile, my old lady knees were regularly aching.

I switched to fitness walking, yoga, aerobics tapes, and weights. I prefer jogging with the dog, but adjusting to our limitations is part of life. My goal is to be healthy and physically fit. Jogging was my first choice, but there are other ways. My knees were just another obstacle to work around. Rarely is success in any endeavor a straight line. How we perceive obstacles and choose to address them can be the difference between success and failure.

Even after treatment, I managed to look like an idiot, especially in the winter. I would put on sweats and tennis shoes. Once Poochy saw the magic shoes, he would bound around me barking wildly. I wore a down jacket that made me look like a big, blue marshmallow. I'd add a fanny pack with a water bottle holder. I'd slide the dog's leash through the fanny pack strap and clipped it to my waist. I'd slip my water baba in the front holder. I added a ski mask, sunglasses, and mittens. By this point the dog was in a frenzy.

Once outside I'd uphold my reputation as the strangest individual in the city. The dog would lead me by the waist. I had a retractable leash and usually Poochy was pretty good. There were occasionally trees he felt required extra sniffing and I'd be yanked backwards when he didn't follow. He'd sometimes crisscross and I'd have to twirl around to get untangled. I referred to that as my dingbat dance. My biggest challenge was keeping an eye out for squirrels and rabbits. If I saw them first and told Poochy, "No," he'd whine, but stay on track. If I said nothing, he would bolt for them, yanking the big blue marshmallow, waist first after him.

Many of us are only interested in God's solutions if His answers conform to our own ideals. My pets provide me with physical affection, companionship, and security — all things I need. The solution I wanted was to get remarried. That is currently not in God's plan for me. It's my attitude that determines whether I appreciate the substitutes God has provided. I have to trust He cares and will provide what is right for me.

We are often certain we know what's best for us. We're like teenagers; we cannot see beyond what we currently want. We get mad at God and figuratively slam the door in His face. I've had many angry conversations with my Father. Honest communication is part of a genuine relationship with anyone. If you read my prayer journal during 1999, you'd be appalled at my anger toward God. I felt attacked and picked on. I wanted Him to take away my problems and fix everything.

That's not how life works. When bad things happen, anger is a natural response. Go ahead and tell God how dangnified you are. He can take it. Share your shattered hopes and dreams. Trust He cares and is crying with you.

Being angry about life's unfairness is not sinful; it's human. It's our responses that get us into trouble. Listen to your Father. I constantly heard: "Hold your tongue," "Stand firm," "Wait patiently," and "Trust Me." None of which I wanted to hear. Short term, I'm often frustrated by God's responses, but long term His answers are always best.

I am willing to act like a fool in order to show my joy in the Lord. Yes, and I am willing to look even more foolish than this.

2 Samuel 6:21b-22a LAB

Chapter 12

Plenty of strong Christians are still constantly worried, angry, and depressed. Assume you have a heart condition and your life is saved with bypass surgery. Afterwards the doctor gives you a diet and exercise program. If you don't follow the doctor's diet and exercise advice, your life has still been saved, but you won't be as healthy.

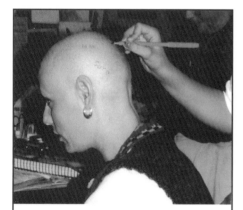

Baldness makes my head a fright,
For it's pale and pasty white.
Add some color, write it in,
Cover up my shiny skin.

The same is true for our faith. It does not exist in a vacuum. You can be saved while having a lower quality of life than Christ intended. Your salvation is not dependent on your attitude. However, the quality of your life and those around you is. As Christians we're supposed to be joyful. The worst advertisement for Christianity is negative believers. If you are constantly joyful, people will notice and want what you have. Attitudes are contagious. How we act is our greatest witness.

When I started dressing up, FirstBorn begged me not to drive to school in my getups, so I didn't. I would never consider embarrassing anyone else. Myself? Absolutely, but not my son. Respect is a part of being positive. If someone else pays the price for your humor, it's not funny. The boys were originally hesitant to tell their friends about my weird getups. By the end, they were proud of me.

They both asked me talk to their classes about my experiences. I brought in a bunch of my costumes. I let the kids try them on and we talked. I taped the verse Philippians 4:4 on the board. We discussed what "Rejoice in the Lord always" meant to me. I let the first and third graders sign or initial my bald head. When the kids signed my head, some could not stop giggling. Others were certain they were doing something wrong and kept asking if it was OK.

During treatment, I spent hours coming up with outfit ideas, finding the items, and writing something to say. Most of the time, I said a line or two. I expanded upon those ideas when I began talking to groups. I had never done any public speaking. The most I'd done was the kids' classes. Nor had I put public speaking on my "to do" list. I felt called to tell others my story. I sent a few letters to cancer support groups, offering to speak for free. Quite frankly, I did not expect much response. Who the heck would want to hear about me? Apparently many groups were desperate for speakers.

The first group wanted me to speak for thirty minutes, yes, half an hour! That's a long time for someone with no experience or training. I figured, given my credentials, they were getting what they paid for. I had no idea how difficult and daunting a thirty-minute speech could be. Being crazy, I said yes.

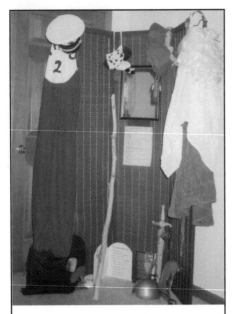

I change behind this trifold screen when I talk. My outline hangs below the mirror. I usually have a table or chair behind me with other costumes on it. With everything I need within reach, I can quickly change and continue speaking.

I had plenty of time to panic...I mean prepare. I wanted to bring my hats and wigs, put them on, and show the audience how silly I looked in treatment. I wrote the speech, but hadn't figured out how to change costumes quickly without losing contact with the audience. I found a $99 trifold room screen with horizontal slats. After I hung a mirror on the screen, made posters, printed handouts, picked up miscellaneous items, and drove to the speaking engagement, I figure it cost me about $125 to speak for free. It was worth every penny. I stepped out in faith and enjoyed speaking.

My first experience wasn't easy. I was extremely nervous. I went to the bathroom about a hundred times beforehand. There were seven women in this small breast cancer support group. I reminded myself not to worry because I'd never see any of them again. I chatted with the members before the meeting. The second person I met was a gray-haired nun. I about died. As a lifelong Catholic, I had an ingrained respect for the clergy. I'd prepared my speech explaining how I'd felt and my personal experiences. My faith reflections were a far cry from traditional convent prayers. I did not want to appear blasphemous.

I was shaking when I was introduced wearing my multicolored "rooster" wig and matching eyelashes. Within minutes I demonstrated how I prayed after I was diagnosed. I basically had a major temper tantrum. I stomped up and down screaming, "Why me" and "It's not fair." Six women laughed and nodded. The nun never cracked a smile.

She didn't laugh when I dressed as Mosezina and read the Ten Chemo Commandments or when I popped out in the conehead and declared God called me to wear it. The rest of the group laughed hysterically. One woman nearly fell out of her chair. (It seems looking and acting stupid really is a personal gift.) In half an hour, I did five deeply religious reflections, and the nun was stone faced. I was so preoccupied with her lack of reactions; I had a hard time focusing on my presentation. I would have skipped certain segments, but I was too inexperienced a speaker. I was afraid if I didn't keep to the script, I'd be lost.

When the meeting was over, I went to the nun to apologize profusely for offending her. Before I could get down on my knees, beg for forgiveness, and promise to do penance, she hugged me and said thank you. It turned out she was too sick from treatment to laugh. She told me my lighthearted approach made her day. Since then, I wish I'd gotten a nun outfit for treatment. The quips I could have done would have been heavenly. Oh well, I'll always regret not getting into the habit.

It is a strange paradox in life, but again and again I realize the more joy I bring others, the more joy I receive. Laughter helps people forget their pain. That's why I like writing humorous pieces. It's no coincidence that I kept a journal and saved my e-mails during 1999. I reviewed both of those when writing this book. I had no idea my reflections would be relevant later, but God did. We are often planting seeds for future callings we aren't aware of yet.

Speaking is an extension of my writing. Giving presentations is a huge high for me, better than any drug. It's not just me; my sons enjoyed it too. They added a dimension I couldn't. They got as many or more laughs than I did. They both used to beg to go, which is odd. How many preteens or teenagers ask to go speak anywhere? Obviously the audience's responses are very rewarding. I am convinced helping others is another secret weapon of happiness. I encourage you to get an automatic *service* revolver and shoot that joy everywhere.

✶✶✶

Where did I get my outfits? Some, like the crusader, the pirate, and the Viking, I pilfered from my children's toy boxes. I purchased the turkey head at a garage sale for fifty cents. Can you believe anyone would sell such a treasure? Others were gifts. Sister Three sent the elephant nose and crazy glasses. Some I created from items around the house. Mosezina was a discarded Santa's beard, my bathrobe, and a stick the boys found. I made the Ten Commandments out of cardboard. A few, like the Scarlet hat and Rudolph nose, I borrowed from friends. Most, I purchased.

Take your problems in jest. If you're joyful in the court of life, your act will impress the King of Kings.

There is a costume store close to the hospital. I'd often swing by after appointments. I got the sombrero, tiara, alien antennas, and conehead there. I was in treatment at Halloween, so I picked up a bunch of costumes on sale after the holiday. Thing Two from Dr. Seuss was about five bucks. My head is so tiny, I was able to buy toddler costumes and only wear the headpieces. Lala the Teletubby, the dog, the flower, and Dot from "A Bug's Life" were all packaged for ages twenty-four months. Each treasure was only two or three dollars. Nothing I got was expensive. It was never about money. It was about being playful and having fun. I encourage you to choose fun so your day-to-day duties don't swallow your joy.

Don't store up treasures here on earth where they can erode away or may be stolen. Store them in heaven where they will never lose their value, and are safe from thieves. If your profits are in heaven your heart will be there too.

Matthew 6:19-21 LAB

Chapter 13

How am I doing now? Great!

I still struggle to make ends meet. I wish I had more time and it's hard being a single parent, but I am happier now than I've ever been. I still have to constantly remind myself to focus on the positive; however, it is easier and often automatic. My lows are never as low. I appreciate the little things more. I try not to take my blessings for granted. I'm also better at determining what is and isn't important. For perspective, I've developed my own unique rating system.

I've been reading "Dear Abby" and "Ann Landers" since I was young. Over the years, it has amazed me how intense people are over trivial topics. At the top of my list is the discussion about how toilet paper should hang off the roll: with the piece to be pulled dangling from the front or from the back. Hello? This is a preference, not an absolute in nature. I cannot understand arguing about, much less taking the time to sit down and write a letter about so inane a subject.

How do I determine if something is a TP issue? If I'd be embarrassed to stand before God, stuttering and stammering, as I explained how I alienated people over so irrelevant a subject, then it is a TP-size problem and should be flushed down the toilet.

I call real issues Holy Toledo-size problems. These are the big-ticket items that everyone agrees create stress, like a tragic death, the loss of a job, divorce, physical ailments, and other such problems. Most of those we're forced to face. There are also easily denied Holy Toledos, like addiction, abuse, chronic deceit, betrayal, or infidelity. Permitting these sins is the same as endorsing them. A denied Holy Toledo affects every member of the family. We are required to address sin because all sin separates us from God.

I know in the past unaddressed Holy Toledos undermined my efforts to be whole and happy. I couldn't be at peace with myself while ignoring

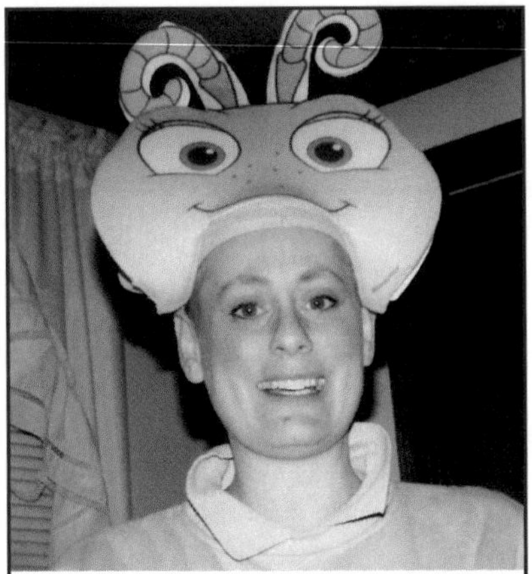

Do small inconveniences bug you? Is your peace of mind stirred up like a hornet's nest over minor irritations like a messy room, being cut off in traffic, or waiting in line? Irrelevant frustrations are like termites. They slowly eat away at our peace. Over time they cause extensive damage. Exterminators say the best defense against termites is to catch them before they're destructive. The same is true with our thoughts. Use a perspective spray on those insect-size irritations. Remind yourself that an extra five minutes in line or on the freeway isn't going to matter tomorrow. Don't allow tiny annoyances to become infestations. Zap those pesky thoughts before they eat away at your joy.

the proverbial elephant in the room. I had to get help. Just as I needed trained experts to remove the cancer in my body, I need trained experts to eradicate the emotional cancers in my life. Don't let pride stop you from getting help and being whole.

I realize most people do not want to take my weird approach to their problems. I don't advocate each of you run out and buy a conehead. It is obviously not right for practically everyone. However, we are all called to be joyous and vigilant about our attitudes. Attitude adjustments require no extra money or time; two things people stretched to the limit do not have. We are not expected to instantly change or become perfect, only to commit to keep trying. Having a positive attitude is not a decision you make once or twice. When you are in a crisis, you may have to refocus your thoughts perpetually. I have some days where I go joyfully along. Most days, I have to redirect my thinking on and off during the day. Some days, it is a constant battle.

One thing is certain, the more I exercise my positive attitude, the easier it overpowers the negative triggers that creep into my consciousness. I was constantly fighting my thoughts, but those days are less and less frequent regardless of the turmoil in my life. It's not realistic to expect to be up every day. What counts is whether your good days vastly outnumber your bad days. Mine didn't used to. Now they do.

Keep what's important in focus.

1999 could have been the worst year of my life. Reflect on what I faced: divorce proceedings, cancer treatment, single parenting, postponing publishing, questionable medical insurance, and financial insecurity. That year, perhaps because life was so bad, I chose to stop surviving and start living and thriving. You can too, and you don't have to wear goofy outfits to do it.

I did not ignore my struggles. Denying problems doesn't make them go away. I kept up with my medical, legal, parenting, and financial responsibilities. There is a big difference between denial and a positive attitude. Pretending an abusive relationship is OK; putting up with an alcoholic partner; accepting perpetual neglect; tolerating lying, stealing, or infidelity, these are NOT signs of a positive attitude. Continuing to allow people to mistreat you is not good or noble. For a response to be positive, it must be healthy and productive, and no amount of laughter can change that.

We all want a fairy godmother, someone who will wave her magic wand, make our problems disappear and our greatest dreams come true. We often turn to God with a fairy godmother attitude. We view our prayer life more like wishing upon a star. When God doesn't grant our wishes, we get frustrated and lose faith. God is not in the wish-granting business. His perspective is eternal. In the faith realm, mice don't instantly become horses. We are supposed to develop our Christian character. God gives us our dreams and He wants to make them a reality, but that requires commitment and sacrifice.

Dreams are not the same as fantasies. A fantasy is unachievable, like me wanting to be a forty plus, female professional football player. In fantasies everything is perfect, everyone likes and admires us, and achievements are easy. Fantasies are never going to happen; no matter how hard we work or what price we're willing to pay, because they are unrealistic.

A dream is something that can realistically be achieved through hard work and acceptable tradeoffs, like going

Invest in your dreams and enjoy the magic.

back to school, changing careers, or becoming an author. God endorses our dreams because He is in the middle of them. Our tradeoffs create challenges, requiring us to trust God.

After cancer treatment, I still had time left on my COBRA health insurance. Even so, I was advised to postpone publishing my novel, *Duty Honor Deceit,* and get a real job (as if writing isn't real work) with predictable pay and medical benefits. After hours of prayer, I rejected that advice.

Our hopes and our dreams make our lives worth living. I'm not living off my writing; I'm living because of it or from it. I get energized whenever I come up with a new prank for my characters, solve a plot problem, think of a one-liner, or write a goofy vignette. It is similar to the runner's high, only thankfully without the sweat.

Our Christian walk should be an adventure we are excited to embrace. God is looking for enthusiastic workers and cheerful givers of their time, talents, and treasures. Too often fear prevents us from achieving our God-given dreams. We are afraid to trust God because we might fail or have to make sacrifices. Our dreams require a leap of faith.

Don't be an "I'm Gonna Goon," always saying that someday I'm gonna do this or I'm gonna do that. I know people who have been miserable in their jobs or with their lives for years, yet after five, ten, fifteen, twenty years of saying they want to change, they never progress beyond the I'm Gonna stage.

There is always a reason why they can't move forward. They are waiting for the perfect situation, at the perfect time, with the perfect offer, and it is always someone else's fault why they don't have it. They want to make no tradeoffs and no sacrifices. Well, hello, reality; none of us get that. If you wait for the perfect situation, you'll go to your grave as an I'm Gonna Goon.

Why? Because God is not in the wish-granting business. He is in the business of miracles. Perfect situations do not require trust in God; sacrifices and risks do. The timing for me to publish wasn't perfect. On the other hand, if my last forty years are any indication, the timing will never be perfect.

If the timing is God's will, the sacrifices will be within acceptable limits, but there are always tradeoffs. I'm not suggesting we ignore our responsibilities and pursue whatever we want. My long-term career goal is to be an author. I would like to be writing fulltime. Unfortunately, life has had other plans. I am now published, definitely a first step, but I'm not even vaguely supporting myself as a writer. Even if I could, as a cancer survivor I cannot currently qualify for private health insurance. My only choice once the COBRA insurance ran out was a group plan through an employer. For five years after treatment, I worked in an emergency room registering patients. No, it's not what I went to college for, but I only had to work 24 hours per week to get health insurance for the boys and myself.

At that time, my career goals were in conflict with my goals as a parent. It's frustrating, but often our individual goals are in conflict with each other. Sometimes we have to trade the good for the best or the short term for the long term. God often guides us to our dreams slowly. Throughout the Bible, God uses challenges to mold people for future callings. We only see the wisdom of certain steps and tradeoffs when we look back.

We also have current responsibilities to fulfill. I will be held accountable for my parenting. The years with my boys were precious and short. I worked the

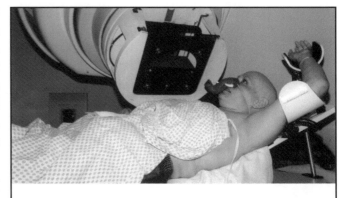

"Joy is not in things, it is in us." —Benjamin Franklin

second shift or graveyard shift. Not my first choice, but the time with my kids was worth it. I was able to work almost exclusively when my boys were with their father. I've pursued my writing and speaking dream slowly, but in the meantime I haven't sacrificed anything I'll regret later.

In 2005, when my boys were older, I decided it was time for a professional career. I took an entry-level job in a brokerage firm. I began at the reception desk taking deposits and supporting the rest of the branch. In December of 2006, I started studying to become a Certified Financial Planner. What I became was certifiable. In the previous 18 months, I had taken and passed three other exams. I thought I knew what I was in for. Yet I had no idea of the quantity of information required. I attended the CFP program at the local university and sat for the ten-hour exam in November 2007.

Between the certification program and the review courses, I had a *few* items to learn: 16 books or 6900 pages of printed material; 6000 PowerPoint slides; 80 hours of DVD lectures; and 75 hours of live class time. I purchased a portable DVD player and relistened to many of the DVDs while I drove to work. I reviewed 975 flash cards, 625 preprinted and 350 I made. I also recorded about seven hours of facts that I played over and over on my iPod. In the last 16 weeks, I answered 2000 practice test questions and spent 325 hours studying.

"If there is no malice in your heart there can be none in your humor." —Will Rogers

This Polly wants a crack-her-up good time. That doesn't include blowing another person's ship out of the water. When engaging in verbal sword play, make certain not to kill someone else's spirit. Good humor takes no prisoners and steals no one's self esteem. Healthy humor lets us laugh at ourselves and our situations without tying another person in knots. Don't force others to walk the plank of pain just to get a laugh. God's secret map of life doesn't lead to one-legged spirits. His treasure chest is filled with jewels of joy and pearls of peace.

At the end, I had a few CFP mind laps reminiscent of chemo brain. Most memorably, just before the test, I took SecondBorn to the ER for stitches. I forgot an obscure bit of his personal information; how to spell his name. He spent weeks thoughtfully reminding me.

I found out I passed the exam in January 2008 and was promoted to Vice President/Financial Consultant a few months later. I had high expectation of finally being financially secure. Too bad I started my practice right as the recession went into full swing. I love helping my clients, but I'm still pinching every penny. There seems to be a misconception in our culture, that if we work hard and do the right thing, we will immediately be rewarded. If that were true, life would be fair, and we all know it isn't. I am dangnified that I worked full-time as a single parent while going back to school and studying 15-20 hours a week, only to find I'm financially no better off. That doesn't mean my CFP is worthless or that I regret doing it. Just that the monetary benefits are vastly delayed.

Our entire culture is focused on instant gratification. The costs are high. We lose the dreaming, planning, and working toward something. Anything we sacrifice and invest in long term becomes exponentially more meaningful. I am confident my current position will lead to financial security at some point. My passion is still writing and speaking. God didn't give me these gifts without a reason. I have to trust His eternal purpose.

For a long time, I had a saying taped to my kitchen cabinet: "Don't trade what you want in the moment for what you want most." I'm sorry I don't know who said that, because it is profoundly true.

I'm trading immediate wealth for untold riches. In my wacky world, there is a big difference between being wealthy and being rich. Money is not bad. Feel free to send more my way. By my definition, wealthy people are interested in money and things they can control. I call it the "Pharisee Complex." They are greedy, self-centered individuals who are always grasping and never satisfied. Pharisees will use any means to get what they want.

Pharisees are focused on people and objects they can buy or get or possess. They view their relationships in terms of what others can do for them. They use people like commodities and leave a trail of pain in their wake. Pharisees sacrifice relationships at home and at work to achieve power, control, status, or wealth. They do not want to cooperate with others, but win at all costs. Their humor is used to insult, gain power, and show superiority. They are focused on the externals of life.

They have fun, but not abiding joy. If externals brought us joy, then people who could afford every pleasure would be deliriously happy. Yet, lots of wealthy people drown their sorrows in drugs, alcohol, and sexual trysts. They have every advantage, engage in nonstop pleasure and are still miserable. Consider Marilyn Monroe, by human standards, she had it all and she committed suicide. Think about how many rich and famous people you can personally name who have ended up in rehab, jail, or committed suicide. Obviously, their fame and wealth did not buy them happiness.

People with the Pharisee Complex may appear to have more on the outside, but they are sick inside where it counts. Trust me, selfish people are not happy people. Their hearts are drained from bitterness, anger, jealousy, lust, and pride and empty hearts make for unhappy individuals. From my unscientific observations, Pharisees are some of the most miserable people on the planet.

Life is about perception. The amount of money someone has is of no significance. People can be living in poverty and be entirely focused on their own selfish desires. By the same token, lots of millionaires are generous, loving individuals. No matter what someone's financial situation, everyone has troubles, relationship problems, and disappointments. What's important for peace and joy is how people deal with the inevitable stumbling blocks in life. Where do they put their trust, in themselves and others or in God?

We're filthy rich and you can be, too!

Put your trust in Christ and work for eternal riches. I'm not suggesting you jump around celebrating a terminal illness or a painful experience. But if you can't change what you're going through, you might as well make the situation as positive as possible. If you could giggle and smile for ten minutes an hour, think what an enormous difference that would have on your mood. Ask God to help you create those ten minutes. They are out there. Christ wants you to be rich and whole in Him.

By my definition rich people invest their energy in activities that enrich everyone's lives, not just their own. They are focused on give-and-take relationships, community service, and helping others, all without causing casualties. They have learned to love and appreciate what they have and not focus on what they don't. The rich spend most of their time on the assets of the heart. They fill their coffers with healthy two-sided relationships. They have family members and friends who share in their triumphs and their trials. They use humor to encourage and cement relationships, not to degrade or shame. They count their blessings, not just their accomplishments.

My life is not perfect and neither am I. I don't have to be. Christ made certain of that. I am focused on eternal treasures and that perspective gives me peace and joy, but it is a constant choice. If your emotional bank account is low, start making positive deposits. A good attitude is the best investment you'll ever make. The assets compound daily, and the return on your investment is endless. You and I may never have money to burn, but I promise you, I am filthy rich, and with God's help, you can be, too.

Ten years later, Jenny is living in Lenexa, KS. She is a Vice President/Financial Consultant for a major brokerage firm and enjoys helping people achieve their financial goals. She continues to write and speak as time permits. Will is a sophomore in college and Jake is a senior in high school. In her free time, Jenny enjoys cooking, yoga and walking the dog.

If you have feedback on *Operation Attitude*, Jenny would love to hear from you at jlissner@HumorFightingCancer.com

Additional copies can be ordered at HumorFightingCancer.com

Other books by J. Lissner

Duty Honor Deceit
A novel

Also available at:

HumorFightingCancer.com

LaVergne, TN USA
25 January 2010
170844LV00005B